LOVE YOURSELF

LOVE YOURSELF

ESSAYS ON SELF-LOVE, CARE AND HEALING INSPIRED BY BTS

EDITED BY

WALLEA EAGLEHAWK AND KERYN IBRAHIM

BULLETPROOF

ISBN 978-0-6450486-3-6 (paperback)
ISBN 978-0-6450486-4-3 (eBook)

Cover design by Paula Pomer

First published in 2021

Bulletproof
Brisbane, Australia
www.bulletproof.revolutionaries.com.au

CONTENTS

RELATED TITLES

Related titles from Bulletproof
   I Am ARMY: It's Time to Begin edited by Wallea Eaglehawk and Courtney Lazore

Related titles from Revolutionaries
   Idol Limerence: The Art of Loving BTS as Phenomena by Wallea Eaglehawk

Related titles from Moonrise
   Through the darkness, I will love myself edited by Wallea Eaglehawk, Nikola Champlin and Padya Paramita

CONTRIBUTORS

Editors

Wallea Eaglehawk is a social theorist, author of *Idol Limerence: The Art of Loving BTS as Phenomena*, and co-editor of both *I Am ARMY: It's Time to Begin* and *Through the darkness, I will love myself*. Alongside her creative practice, Wallea is the CEO and Editor-in-Chief of Revolutionaries, and imprints Bulletproof and Moonrise. A scholar of limerence, identity, love, and BTS, Wallea identifies as a practising revolutionary. Find her on Twitter, Instagram, and Medium @walleaeaglehawk.

Keryn Ibrahim is a writer and academic from Brunei Darussalam. Her interests range from mapping and critical geographies to gender and feminism. Nowadays she aspires to become a professor of BTS, gender, and critical studies, while dabbling in poetry and creative writing on the side. You can find her on Twitter @kerynibrahim.

Contributors

Jasmine Proctor is a writer, researcher, amateur astrologer, and a lifelong fangirl. Within the realm of academics, her interests lie at the intersection of fan studies and political economic theory, an area she is currently pursuing in her graduate research. Outside of scholarship, Jasmine is an ARMY, an avid supporter of all forms of fan content, and a plant mum. Find her on Twitter, Instagram, and Medium @iamjazzrae.

Gabrielle Punzalan is a writer from the suburbs of Atlanta, Georgia currently studying at Kennesaw State University. Her work can be found in the Moonrise companion to *Love Yourself, Through the darkness, I will love myself*. She enjoys writing stories and dreams of publishing her own book one day. Find her on Twitter @GabbyS_Pun and Instagram @gabby_s.p.

Rashifa Aljunied is a student of international relations at the National University of Malaysia. Her interests are watching documentaries and staying up to date on international affairs. She started writing after being inspired by BTS' storytelling of hope and despair. She is a passionate advocate actively campaigning for climate change. You can find her on Twitter @youngaljunied.

Devin Barney, M.A. is a scholar at the intersection of community, cultural, and developmental psychology. His work explores topics of socialisation and development within multicultural spaces. Devin is a U.S. nomad who enjoys exploration and travel, novel culinary experiences, and the challenge of inhabiting multiple time zones at once. He also loves love and romance, a good bildungsroman, and happy crying. He is on Twitter @PsychofBTS and Instagram @barndorable.

Brunna Martins is a Brazilian writer, reviewer, and student of journalism. She is also a fan studies scholar, who is currently developing a book about BTS, ARMY, and communication with young people in the digital age. Find her on Twitter @brusmb_twt, Instagram @brusmb_ig and Medium @brunnasmb.

Cindy Nguyen (Như Quỳnh) is a trisector innovator who seeks multi-faceted, transformative change. She is the creator of Cereus Context, an educational resource that supports the contextualisation of social issues and nuanced understanding. Find her on Twitter, Instagram, and Medium @cereus_context.

Jacinta Bos is a freelance artist from Tasmania, Australia. Other than BTS, she is passionate about foreign culture and her emerging photography career. Find her on Twitter and Instagram @jacinta_bos.

Raneem Iftekhar is a teenage student from Southern California currently preparing for university to study environmental policy and economics. She is passionate about creating and consuming any form of art, from painting to music and dancing. In the unexpected time alone due to the pandemic, she made a long-held dream a reality and started her own small business with her art inspired by the natural world and BTS, among other things. You can find her and her art on Instagram @moonlight_and_ferns.

Destiny Harding is an artist and writer based in Canberra, Australia. She is currently studying Asia-Pacific culture, digital humanities, and linguistics while maintaining a keen interest in fandom and BTS. *Love Yourself* and its companion book (*Through the darkness, I will love myself*) are her first contributions to Revolutionaries and their imprints but hopefully not the last! You can find her on Twitter and Instagram @jungefh.

Shelley Hoani is a strong Māori woman from Aotearoa/New Zealand. She celebrates her many roles in life as a mother/grandmother, educator, Indigenous researcher, and healer. As an ARMY you'll find her online with Borasaek Vision and Bangtan Academy. As an aspiring author, poet, and artist, you'll find her contributions nestled in the pages of The R3 Journal, Dream Glow, Borasaek Vision Magazines, and now, Bulletproof. Twitter is her main social media platform @Shells131065, in reality though wherever her heart feels nourished, that's where you'll find her.

TWO WORDS, THREE SYLLABLES, TWELVE LETTERS: INTRODUCING LOVE YOURSELF

Wallea Eaglehawk

I was going through a pretty down period in my life. It was about four years ago, and I just decided to have a vulnerable moment and put one of those thought-provoking journal entries out on Twitter. Four years ago when I started this, a lot of them were about self-love because I was going through that down period realising that I didn't consider myself enough. Amazingly enough, talk about wonderful timing and just being ready for an opportunity, the very popular group BTS had just released an album called *Love Yourself*. So I put out all these messages of self-love and I'm thinking "this is not going to be a good idea" because this big, larger than life sixteen time WWE champion is now talking about vulnerability and the fact that you are enough and you shouldn't be ashamed of who you are. But it caught fire because of the BTS ARMY. I was essentially sending a similar message as the band, and these books exist because the BTS ARMY were brave enough to support my vulnerable moment. [...] I've really got to thank K-pop, I've really got to thank BTS for supporting me in a moment of weakness.

— John Cena on how he came to
write two books about self-love[1]

BTS, short for 방탄소년단, Bangtan Sonyeondan — in English, Bulletproof Boyscouts — are a seven-member K-pop (Korean pop) group from South Korea. The members are 김남준, Kim Namjoon, *RM*; 김석진, Kim Seokjin, *Jin*; 민윤기, Min Yoongi, *Suga*; 정호석, Jung Hoseok, *j-hope*; 박지민, Park Jimin, *Jimin*; 김태형, Kim Taehyung, *V*; and, 전정국, Jeon Jungkook; *Jung Kook*.

Since their debut in 2013, the group has continued to gain in popularity, topical examples are a recent Grammy nomination and performance,[2] and being named the top recording artist in the world in 2020.[3] Their influence both in Korea and globally is widespread and intrinsically linked to the group's artistry, performance, authenticity, and above all else, their message.

When giving an introduction to BTS, it is important to acknowledge their fans: ARMY. You see, BTS and ARMY are somewhat of a package deal. Though, of course, their music can be enjoyed without the knowledge of or engagement with ARMY, BTS would be the first to say that they wouldn't be where they are today without their fans. As such, you can't venture too far into the world of BTS before coming across an ARMY, or hearing about ARMY, or perhaps even becoming one yourself. To understand ARMY is to understand BTS, and vice versa. In my previous anthology co-edited with Courtney Lazore, *I Am ARMY: It's Time to Begin*, when introducing ARMY, I wrote:

> It can be difficult to summarise ARMY in so few words; they are a true cross-section of the world. Or, perhaps it would be better to describe them as a microcosm of humankind — a mikrokosmos if you like. ARMY numbers are estimated to be in the range of 20-30 million; they are the most visible fandom on Earth. [...]
>
> Through the internet, ARMY has been able to grow and prosper. Through this, ARMY has propelled BTS to new heights with collectivised actions such as streaming and voting parties. There are no hard and fast rules to becoming or being an ARMY; no age limit, no prerequisites. The only criterion is that ARMY must love BTS, every member, no matter what.[4]

At this point, you might be wondering why BTS and ARMY are being introduced in a book that promises essays on the lived experience and practise of self-love and care. If that's the case, then never fear, you are most definitely in the right place. Earlier I mentioned that BTS are where they are today in large part due to their message. There are, of course, many messages that BTS has disseminated through their music and beyond. But there has been one particular message, theme, exploration, that has played a pivotal role in their success. Even more so, it has played a pivotal role in the lives of their fans, ARMY, and the broader global community. This is why it's so important to introduce both BTS and ARMY as co-conspirators, partners, collaborators — this is not only the origin story of this book, but of a movement that exists in the hearts and minds of upwards of 20 million people around the world.

Two words, three syllables, twelve letters. Love yourself. Say them out loud right now as you read them and you might be confused, much like I was when I first heard them. But say them while looking at yourself in the mirror with unwavering eye contact, and perhaps you'll start to understand what adventure is afoot. Perhaps you're already in the thick of it. Either way, it can't hurt to say it. Once more, for the sake of art:

Love yourself.

> 어제의 나 오늘의 나 내일의 나
> Yesterday's me, today's me, tomorrow's me
> (*I'm learning how to love myself*)
> 빠짐없이 남김없이 모두 다 나
> Without exception, all together, they are all me
> — *Answer: Love Myself*, BTS[5]

I vividly remember the first time I heard the call to love myself from BTS. I was a few weeks into being an ARMY in early 2019 when I came across a Jimmy Fallon interview where the group were promoting their latest album *Love Yourself: Answer*. RM explained that BTS' message — the one which they had just shared at the United Nations General Assembly — is "speak yourself" which is part of a "love yourself" journey.[6] He added that in order to truly love ourselves we must know who we are, where we're from — we must find our voice in order to speak ourselves so that no one else can speak over us or for us.[6]

At that moment, I was equal parts intrigued and two degrees shy of utterly dismissive. First and foremost, I wanted to know more about this message of self-love. But secondly, and of more interest to me then, and now as I reflect, I was frustrated by such a call. How can someone say four words — love yourself, speak yourself — and expect that I, and many others, will heed the directive? Is self-love not an incredibly complex concept that is deeply personal and often highly political? "Love myself?" I scoffed, "oh yes sure, that's easy, thanks for the tip."

As I continued down the rabbit hole of BTS videos eagerly provided by the YouTube algorithm that day, I began to realise the subtle quality of a celebrity saying those two — or rather, four — words without further explanation. In the space of time between watching the Fallon interview and wherever I was when the realisation hit me, I had engaged in a heated dialogue with my many inner-selves on what self-love looks like on individual, interpersonal, community, structural, political, and global levels.

It was here that I realised that BTS saying "love yourself" was the spark, and ARMY, of which I was now one, was the fan to the flame. First, within their own individual understandings, and then spreading outwards — perhaps mimicking the same process as BTS which inevitably comes to the point of outreach, which was where I, like many countless others, much like John Cena from the start of this chapter, was able to become one with the fiery movement.

> 내가 나인 게 싫은 날 영영 사라지고 싶은 날
> On a day you hate being yourself, on a day you want to disappear forever,
> 문을 하나 만들자 너의 맘 속에다
> let's build a door in your mind
> 그 문을 열고 들어가면 이 곳이 기다릴 거야

> Once you open the door and enter, this place will wait
> for you
> 믿어도 괜찮아 널 위로해줄 Magic Shop
> It's okay to believe *Magic Shop* that will comfort you
> — *Magic Shop*, BTS[7]

Over the coming weeks and months I learnt more and more about BTS' message of self-love through my experience as a fan. Though I was initially put off by the simplicity of the directive of "love yourself", I soon came to realise that the nuanced understanding I was looking for absolutely existed. But instead of a handbook or an instructional video, the journey towards understanding BTS' message of self-love required me to become a fan and learn through an appreciation of their craft. I had to come to a place where I was open to letting them lead me, walk with me, and show me their journey while allowing me space to reflect on my own.

What I came to learn through being an ARMY, enjoying BTS' music, and observing not only the fandom but myself as a fan, is that the love that BTS explores in their lyrics is a revolutionary love, a love that is a doing word. It's not passive, rather love asks of everyone to seek change. Firstly of themselves, then of their worlds.

> Maybe I made a mistake yesterday, but yesterday's me is still me. I am who I am today, with all my faults. Tomorrow I might be a tiny bit wiser, and that's me, too. These faults and mistakes are what I am, making up the brightest stars in the constellation of my life. I have come to love myself for who I was, who I am, and who I hope to become.
> — RM, United Nations General Assembly[8]

The Love Yourself era was profound for both BTS and ARMY which saw the group start to gain traction in the west, especially in the United States. The era encompassed BTS' trilogy of albums *Love Yourself: Her* (2017), *Love Yourself: Tear* (2018), and *Love Yourself: Answer* (2018); subsequent tours of Love Yourself (2018-2019) and Speak Yourself (2019); BTS' Love Myself campaign with UNICEF to end violence towards children; BTS' speech at the 73rd session of the UN General Assembly in 2018, and; the countless televised performances, tweets, VLives and other forms of communication from the group throughout this time. This introduction doesn't seek to chronicle and analyse the era in its entirety, nor does this book, rather this is to give context to what continues to be BTS' most influential message to date.

Through their *Love Yourself* trilogy — *Her, Tear,* and *Answer* — BTS explored the many kinds of love that one experiences in life. As the name might suggest, the answer to that unknown question is that first you must learn to love yourself before loving others. The driving force behind the concept can be found in the lyrics of *Answer: Love Myself*: "perhaps, than loving someone else, it is more difficult to love myself."[5] Make no mistake, the catalyst for this message and movement isn't rooted in an egotistical self-love that comes from being an adored idol. Rather, it's quite the opposite. Which adds further gravitas to such an easily delivered prompt of "love yourself" — both idol, fan, and curious onlooker are equals in this quest from self-hate, or at least apathy, towards actualisation and love. Better yet, this is a journey not simply shared *from* BTS to ARMY and beyond, but one that exists *between* the two. This is why the message of "love yourself" has been so impactful in the lives of ARMY around the world, because it has been a shared experience with a group they love and adore. One without end, as it continues on to this day.

> You've shown me I have reasons
> I should love myself
> 내 숨 내 걸어온 길 전부로 답해
> I answer with all my breath and all the path I've walked
> along
> — *Answer: Love Myself*, BTS[5]

The strongest message throughout BTS' work is love, but it is also one of the most nuanced ones. Often, it's overt, such as the title of their entire *Love Yourself* trilogy. But also it's more subtle with lyrics like "when you called me, I became your flower"[9] which, according to translator Doolset, refers to the famous Korean poem *The Flower* by Kim Choonsoo, where "giving a name to someone symbolises love".[10] BTS use the metaphor of flowers throughout their work, as well as revisiting the notion of name giving as symbolic of love. BTS' nuanced take on love can be seen many ways, for example, with lyrics such as "I throw all of myself into this two-sided world"[11] which shows a love for their art; "seven summers and cold winters, and more to come"[12] which shows a love for friends; "I didn't even have a name, before I met you"[13] which revisits *The Flower* to represent a love for ARMY, and, lastly; "no matter what kinds of waves strike, we will endlessly sing towards you"[14] which shows a deep love for humankind. Lastly, the concept of love and identity is deeply intertwined in the world of BTS; reflecting how love is a microcosm of the self, and vice versa. Of course, it must be noted that these interpretations of lyrics are my own. That is the beauty of art after all, is it not?

All of this is to say, according to BTS, to be human is to love; humans are love in physical form. Both BTS and ARMY were created, and remain continuously united in love. Love that is complex and nuanced at times, but also a love that is pure which is able to transcend cultural, language, and physical barriers. Love is BTS' call to action, they ask of us to learn to love ourselves and to warmly embrace others in whatever way we can. This message has transcended the Love Yourself era alone and exists throughout all of their work, as their work has always been a reflection of their most genuine selves; and their journey has always been towards authenticity and self-love.

> 빛나는 나를 소중한 내 영혼을
> The shining me, the precious soul of mine
> 이제야 깨달아 So I love me
> I realise only now, so I love me
> 좀 부족해도 너무 아름다운 걸
> Though I'm not perfect, I'm so beautiful
> I'm the one I should love in this world
>
> — Epiphany, BTS[15]

I hope by now I have demonstrated why it is that I am introducing BTS and ARMY in a book of essays about self-love. By all means, this is a book inspired by BTS' Love Yourself era which continues to impact the lives of millions of people around the world today. I truly believe there is no one else in the realm of music, with influence like that of BTS, that is sharing such a nuanced, complex, and powerful message right now. Which is why I felt it timely to create a book that shows the application of BTS' "love yourself, speak yourself" message in everyday life, alongside my co-editor

Keryn Ibrahim who shares my excitement in merging the realms of fandom, scholarship, and writing.

There is another book that accompanies this one already out in the world, *Through the darkness, I will love myself* which is responding to the Love Yourself era with works of poetry and prose. This is to reflect the multifaceted experience of the era, the experience of self-love itself, and of course, the multitalented fandom that is ARMY. One book is simply not enough, nor is *Love Yourself* the be all and end all of books that are inspired by or discuss this era through such a lens as autoethnography or personal essays — though it is the first. If you are interested in learning more about the ARMY identity and experience, I do recommend reading *I Am ARMY: It's Time to Begin* which can provide further context for *Love Yourself* and serve as a great introduction to the BTS phenomenon for those who are curious onlookers — and, of course, it's recommended to those at any point in their ARMY journey.

Amongst these pages you will find a range of experiences and stories that share universal themes and truths. Some may be familiar to you, some may be new. These stories are not about BTS even as all the contributors are ARMY and have been deeply influenced by the group and fandom alike. The stories are personal accounts of the writers' lives that are linked to socio-cultural-political analyses and understandings for further context and, perhaps, to provide the reader with tools for understanding their own journey, too. Each writer has approached the task of writing an autoethnography differently, and as such the concept of autoethnography is expanded and played with — some are conventional, some are not. All provide a heartfelt examination of self-love as a journey, a work in progress.

In the first essay, Jasmine Proctor explores the dichotomy of her passions, exploring the tensions of being both a Marxist and an ARMY. In the second essay, Gabrielle Punzalan uses the concept of the broken vase theory to tell the story of her journey towards self-love. Rashifa Aljunied gives an insight into how she resists and transforms the stigma she experiences while seeking a diagnosis for her invisible illness in essay three. In the fourth essay, Devin Barney uses the concept of illusory truth to help rewrite his life as an Asian American. In the fifth essay, Brunna Martins shares the story of how she learnt to love herself, with the help of BTS, after sexual assault. In essay six, Cindy Nguyen shares the story of her inherently radical existence as a perpetual foreigner and the acts of self-care and resistance which she has learnt and cultivated over time. In the seventh essay, Jacinta Bos shares her journey with being alienated from her persona in high school and being a young adult with acne, to now being able to face herself and all her complexities. Raneem Iftekhar in essay eight explores her relationship with self-love through the process of painting a self-portrait — with layers of persona, shadow, and ego. In the ninth essay, Destiny Harding analyses her disordered eating and how she's building a nurturing relationship with herself on a wavering journey of self-love. In the tenth and final essay, Shelley Hoani follows her footsteps home in a moving piece that blends Māori knowledge, her life's journey, and the experience of being an ARMY. Lastly, my co-editor Keryn Ibrahim will reflect on resilience and hope in the conclusion.

No summary can do these stories justice, but it is only right that I introduce the contributions that make up this important body of work. It has been an honour and a privilege to work alongside my co-editor Keryn to bring these essays into the world. I am grateful to each of the contributors for working tirelessly on their chapters, and for the joy we have been able to share in the process.

These essays don't seek to define self-love, rather, they show self-love in action. Further, they show self-love on a spectrum of feelings and experiences that often oscillate from apathy to self-hate and beyond. Throughout this book, the reasons for why these experiences exist on a level that are not only personal, but political, are analysed and critiqued. Such as the experiences of Asian Americans, immigrants, and Indigenous peoples, which have deep roots in systemic racism, patriarchy, and colonialism. Through this, the resilience that comes from a long-upheld, active resistance to oppression shines through as a beacon of hope — showing the way forward.

These essays exist to remind you, dear reader, that you are not alone. No matter what your personal circumstances may be, no matter what your journey looks like right now. Here is a book written by twelve people from around the world who are walking this path with you. Wherever this journey may take us, I look forward to being by your side.

Content warnings
Essay five contains discussions of sexual assault and violence; essay nine contains discussions of disordered eating, and; essay ten contains mentions of physical, emotional, and sexual abuse.

Throughout this book there are analyses and discussions, often accompanying descriptions of experiences, that centre around mental health, racism, sexism, gender bias and other forms of oppression.

References

[1]   TheEllenShow. (2021). *John Cena credits BTS Army for supporting his journey to self-love.* [Video]. YouTube. https://www.youtube.com/watch?v=NW4lwYHh7qY

[2]   Mcintyre, H. (2021, March 11). *BTS's Grammy nomination is a huge milestone, but music's biggest night still hasn't really honored K-pop.* https://www.forbes.com/sites/hughmcintyre/2021/03/11/btss-grammy-nomination-is-a-huge-milestone-but-musics-biggest-night-still-hasnt-really-honored-k-pop/?sh=733501bc559e

[3]   Mcintyre, H. (2021, March 4). *BTS have officially been named the top recording artist in the world in 2020.* https://www.forbes.com/sites/hughmcintyre/2021/03/04/bts-have-officially-been-named-the-top-recording-artists-in-the-world-in-2020/?sh=331673002487

[4]   Eaglehawk, W. (2020). Enter the magic shop: Introducing I am ARMY. In W. Eaglehawk & C. Lazore (Eds.), *I am ARMY: It's time to begin.* Bulletproof.

[5]   BTS. (2018). Answer: Love myself [Song]. On *Love yourself: Answer.* Big Hit Entertainment; Doolset. (2018). *Answer: Love myself* [Translation]. https://doolsetbangtan.wordpress.com/2018/08/24/answer-love-myself/

[6]   The Tonight Show Starring Jimmy Fallon. (2018). *Jimmy interviews the biggest boy band on the planet BTS | The tonight show.* [Video]. https://youtu.be/W4mmfzFazoI

[7]   BTS. (2018). Magic shop [Song]. On *Love yourself: Answer.* Big Hit Entertainment; Doolset. (2018). *Magic shop* [Translation]. https://doolsetbangtan.wordpress.com/2018/06/01/magic-shop/

8 BTS. (2018). *BTS speech at the United Nations/UNICEF* [Video]. https://youtu.be/oTe4f-bBEKg

9 BTS. (2018). Serendipity [Song]. On *Love yourself: Answer*. Big Hit Entertainment; Doolset. (2018). *Serendipity* [Translation]. https://doolsetbangtan.wordpress.com/2018/08/24/serendipity/

10 Doolset. (2018). *Serendipity*. https://doolsetbangtan.wordpress.com/2018/08/24/serendipity/

11 BTS. (2020). ON [Song]. On *Map of the soul: 7*. Big Hit Entertainment; Genius. (2020). *BTS - ON (English translation)* [Translation]. https://genius.com/Genius-english-translations-bts-on-english-translation-lyrics

12 BTS. (2020). 친구 (Friends) [Song]. On *Map of the soul: 7*. Big Hit Entertainment; Doolset. (2020). 친구 (Friends) [Translation]. https://doolsetbangtan.wordpress.com/2020/02/21/friends/

13 BTS. (2020). Moon [Song]. On *Map of the soul: 7*. Big Hit Entertainment; Doolset. (2020). *Moon* [Translation]. https://doolsetbangtan.wordpress.com/2020/02/22/moon/

14 BTS. (2020). Louder than bombs [Song]. On *Map of the soul: 7*. Big Hit Entertainment; Doolset. (2020). *Louder than bombs* [Translation]. https://doolsetbangtan.wordpress.com/2020/02/21/louder-than-bombs/

15 BTS. (2020). Epiphany [Song]. On *Love yourself: Answer*. Big Hit Entertainment; Doolset. (2020). *Epiphany* [Translation]. https://doolsetbangtan.wordpress.com/2018/08/09/epiphany/

A DICHOTOMY OF PASSION

Jasmine Proctor

Intro: Resistance as ritual

"What was it that radicalised you?"

It was a simple tweet, a simple question I had stumbled upon through my endless hours of late night timeline scrolling. It was simple and yet it made me pause. Because I didn't really know.

Hastily, I scrolled through the replies, scouring the varying instances that led to a plethora of class revelations and awakenings. Of course there were dozens of answers; there are always different flints to start different flames, but they all lead to the same result: a fire. For some it was entering academia, falling upon key texts like *Capital* and *The Communist Manifesto* or taking a class on Frankfurt School theory. For others, it was that moment of struggle in working-class experience, a conflict or a clash or an uprising, that made them realise the true power struggles that riddle our reality.

I always thought I fell into that latter category, but I guess it doesn't really fit. The question itself, I found, doesn't really fit.

Because it wasn't a moment. No, as I continued through the copious responses in search of something that would stick, I realised that it wasn't a sudden spark that started my revolutionary spirit. There was no pilot light, a switch turned on and the sudden blaze burning forth. Rather, I came to realise that my radicalisation started from the very beginning. And it was instilled in me through a crucial element in working-class life: music.

My dad always believed music was going to lead the revolution. I think it was instilled in me from the very beginning that being working class and a lover of rock n' roll was something that went hand in hand. Music is often regarded as a legitimating factor in any subculture, but within working-class circles it becomes less of a process of authentication and more a way of life.[1] For my dad, it was an outlet. Music was both an escape from the current conditions and a means through which he saw his beliefs being enacted. My dad was (and is) a *fan*, for all intents and purposes of the word. And it's something he still holds with pride. It's something defiant. Being a fan, an ardent follower of Queen, The Doors, The Guess Who, and so many other artists is something that proudly symbolises his working-class identity. The CDs and tapes that lined our walls during my childhood were simultaneously emblems of defiance and signs of collective identity. My dad's fanship moved him even into the realm of putting that revolutionary presence into action, leading a band that played local gigs and belting out the songs that define who he is. This is his revolutionary act — expressing his fanship through enactment and participating in his own fan community, in his own way. For him, music is the movement.

Under capitalism, alienation of the self from labour and solidarity is the key ingredient to making the machine run.[2-4] That individualised need to produce, to compete, and to challenge that defines neoliberal understandings of how capital operates under the current system drives a wedge between who we are and who society wants us to be. In my father's claim to fan identity and passion towards the music he selected to represent himself, he engages in an active fight against this notion. Fan scholar Mark Duffet[5] explains that being a fan is not a passive action; fans select, engage, recreate, and reinterpret texts in order to construct their own identity.[6-8] More than anything, being a fan is being part of a *collective*.[5,9] The sheer act of identifying with a fan community, branding yourself with the crest of your fan object and stating that you are a part of this group, is in and of itself a revolutionary practice. It's resistant. It's defiant. But seeing that, especially through the lens of Marxist theories of labour and commodity fetishism, is difficult. It's even harder when you identify as female, navigating the space of not only where you stand in relation to capital, but also the patriarchal values that make that system run. Balancing the fine line between feminist, working-class praxis and fan consumption is sometimes impossible. It's a difficult dichotomy to rectify, one which makes the process of loving yourself not quite as linear.

Girls just wanna to have fun

It's easy to see, then, how my identity as a fan was almost inevitable. I cannot remember a time when I wasn't in love with something, bright, coloured walls lined with posters and cutouts of my favourite artists from day one. It was almost like I came out of the womb branded a fan, constantly obsessed with a musician or a book or a film. It became a defining feature of my identity, one that I never questioned in my early childhood years. Growing up, fanship, if anything, was eagerly encouraged, being the daughter of an avid follower of Freddie Mercury and a lover of all things Melissa Etheridge. Saturday mornings were spent belting out the lyrics of *Hammer to Fall*, my dad and I giving our best Freddie impersonations as we polished the coffee table. Evening car rides were to the sapphic tune of *Come to My Window*, the longing for a love my adolescent mind couldn't quite comprehend bleeding into the raindrops racing down my backseat window. Music and fanship was *feeling*. It permeated the spaces of my childhood, settling into the crevices and filling the gaps that working-class life left. It became ingrained in my being; it was, like my parents, who I was.

I navigated grade school with the idea that everyone held this same belief. Everyone was a fan. Everyone had *something* they loved. Because how could they not? But the reality of my experience as an anomaly quickly set in one day, in the first grade, when an oh-so-kind classmate taught me a brand-new word: obsessed.

Kids liked things, sure. Beyblades, Pokemon, Sailor Moon, or Britney Spears. They liked them the same way adults liked Costco samples or *Dateline*. They would play with them, get excited when friends brought up the topic. But as soon as it was over, as soon as the card battle was won or CD had finished, they would move on. Turn off the TV, put the toys down, or eject the album, and move on. It wasn't a part of their identity. They just liked it; they weren't obsessed. Obsessed meant excess. Obsessed meant compulsion. Obsessed meant infatuation. Obsessed was a bad word.

I couldn't understand it. Didn't they feel it? That pressure on the heart, the physical sensation that boils in your upper chest when you listen to a song or read a book or watch a film. That pull

33

to *know* more, because this piece of media or person just aligns to your soul. That indescribable feeling that keeps you up at night, turning page after page or playing song after song. It lights up your nervous system, settles into your ribcage and takes your heart captive. Like this person or character just *gets* it. They *are* it. That process of becoming one with something to the point where the boundaries between you and it are indistinguishable. Where you're unable to think, feel, or do anything that isn't related to it. And you *want* that. You need it, with every cell and every fibre.

Didn't they feel it too?

But they didn't. They didn't know and they didn't get it. They didn't get *me*. Add in the fact that I was also a *girl*? Now that right there was an equation that translated to yet another word of choice: irrational. It was a tale as old as time, a stereotype that spanned generations and embedded itself into the collective understanding of female passion. From the rabid Beatles fans of the 1960s, to the delusional Backstreet Boys fangirls of the 1990s — mainstream media has rarely favoured girls and their expression of love. While Joli Jensen[10] has described this as a pathologised fan identity, where being a fan is viewed as a psychological disorder, fan studies scholar Suzanne Scott[11] recognises that this stereotype is used exclusively against female passions. Sound familiar? It's because our society is rooted in a patriarchal system that has always hated female emotion, dating back to the historical classification of female "hysteria".[12] There is a history here, a history that impacted the very contemporary reality of my childhood. It, like with any identity that does not fit within society's norms, becomes a classifier. It became a label. And labels, as we know, stick.

I tried my best to stick it out, to try and embrace this new-found title like a badge of honour. But it inevitably grew with each passing year, this new feeling that I came to recognise as shame. As feminist scholar Sarah Ahmed explains, it's because shame is a sticky emotion; it clings to our interactions and transfers itself from one relation to the next.[13] Like a child's sticky hands, it adhered to anything I touched or said, an ickiness that I couldn't scrub off. I began to feel ashamed of who I was and embarrassed about my excess. I began, I now know, to hate the parts of me I had been raised to love.

The shame from school only added to the struggles I was experiencing mentally from issues at home. Because growing up working class brings with it its own set of trauma, I discovered. No one tells you of the generational issues that stem from poverty, the impacts it has on your parents and their relationship. Not when you're 5 or 10 or sometimes even 20. No one tells you that when the divorce hits, the depression follows shortly after. No one tells you that it doesn't leave, that it will morph and twist and turn inside of you, manifesting in eating disorders, panic attacks, and, most of all, self-hatred. No one tells you that when you're a child, it's hard to love yourself as it is, but trauma and the alienation from your peers only makes the process that much more difficult. And no one tells you that once your mental health begins to spiral, it's hard to embrace and cherish those parts of you that make you who you are. It's hard to grasp onto your passions when your world is falling apart, hard to wear your heart on your sleeve when it's broken without your consent. I couldn't find the will to fight against labels when I was already fighting myself.

But fandom in private was an escape even if it did bring me shame in public. I needed it. When my heart felt its heaviest, Britney reminded me that I was stronger than yesterday, that loneliness could be a superpower. Nights were spent on my bedroom floor, drowning out the constant stream of arguments below by finding consolation in the words of P!nk's *Family Portrait*. When my inner thoughts felt their most inescapable, Gwen was there, her fantastical world an escape that I would turn to with just the press of a button. Whether it was posting Arashi fanfiction as a teen on LiveJournal or consuming Panic! At the Disco's *A Fever You Can't Sweat Out* on repeat while my now-single mum picked up the pieces of our lives, I found consolation in my fan practices; it was what scholar Penelope Eate describes as a means to express creative liberty, free from the constraints of trauma and shame.[15] There was a space there, a space that was not present in the physical reality my younger self faced. Unbeknownst to myself, mapping out a territory within the terrain of adolescence through fanship was a winning of space through resistance,[14] even if it was merely within the four walls of my bedroom. Even if it was just between my best friend and I. Even if I was still fighting to love who I was with my world falling apart around me. Even if it was hard.

Comrade fangirl

Little by little, I was able to cleanse myself of shame's residue, but I entered the academic world of higher education wearing these experiences on my sleeve. I was still struggling with the mind battles of before, but now my iPod was loaded with Big Bang's discography, those hateful thoughts being deliberately drowned out by the sound of *Haru Haru* on repeat. I charged head first into my communications studies degree with the hopes of finding my passions validated, somewhere or by someone. And they were. At least, for a bit.

It's often said that theory is nothing without practice, but for me, I realised, it was the opposite. Of course I fell in love with my degree, reveled in the ability to study both K-pop (*can you believe?*) and Victorian literature (I might've taken on a joint English major my third year). Both schools of thought brought with them ventures into issues of power, distribution of wealth, and, of course, an understanding of society. But it was the end of my fourth year that truly marked the beginning of a beautiful discovery, one that would set the foundation of my world view in years to come: Marxism. Developed from the works of German philosophers Karl Marx and Friedrich Engels, Marxism is a socioeconomic theory that critically analyses how society is structured around class, labour, and the uneven distribution of wealth. Suddenly, I realised as I sat in the middle of the seminar classroom, it made sense. Suddenly it felt like my childhood experiences of class struggle were legitimated. Like Dorothy leaving her sepia-hued Kansas reality and entering the technicolour land of Oz, it was an awakening.

But just as they were put into perspective, they also felt incomplete. Because, upon closer inspection, wasn't I actively engaging in my own exploitation through being a fan? Critical media scholar Mark Andrejevic understands the role of fans in mainstream media as loyal followers, promoters of consumer culture who, even in their performance of agency through the reproduction of texts, still find themselves stuck within the clutches of the capitalist framework.[16] In the eyes of my communication studies degree, fans and audiences were not resistant, but rather implicit in their own deception. I quickly began to realise that my ideology and my identity were like two opposite sides of a magnet.

Because how could I be anti-capitalist while also being a fan?

In graduate school, I realised that academia was a lot like grade school. There stood a surprisingly opaque, yet undiscussed barrier between those rabid fans and true appreciation: being a *fanatic* versus an *aficionado*.[10] Only this time, it wasn't based on the notion of gender (or at least not explicitly) but rather on *taste*; on class and restraint. The aficionado was an area untainted by commodity culture, rich in what sociologist Pierre Bourdieu defines as cultural capital, aka knowing the right things and behaving the right way that gives one status in a certain social circle.[17] This afforded academics the luxury of observing. It was a title that allowed for analysis of the fanatics, where barriers were upheld in the name of critique.

I was not an aficionado — I was a fan. I had taken my obsession too far, to the point of pursuing it as a degree. Like the labels of grade school, it too stuck, a brand that trailed with me into each class, each interaction, and each conference. It became what sociologist Erving Goffman explains as stigma, an identifiable blemish that I could not mask.[18] It defined my interactions, materialised in the awkward nods after I disclosed my research interests to peers, crept into the hesitant smiles of faculty upon hearing my paper topics. And I wasn't the only one; several of my peers were also fans of different things. But it was the stigma that held them back from gushing over the latest music video, cautious that the tiniest bit of excess would leak out. That they would be caught. That they would be viewed as less academic for being a *fangirl*. Again, that nagging feeling of self-despise began to grow. Throughout my years of university, I had actively used my fanship to overcome my childhood trauma, wielding it like a crutch to get me through depressive episodes. And yet here I was, back to square one and covered with sticky handprints of shame.

But an understanding of stigma also acts as an understanding of identity — how the embracing of a stigmatising label can counterly act as an identity symbol. Subcultural theorists have often looked at how members of groups like fan communities congregate around the meaning of a particular object or marker, and how that translates into what sociologist Dick Hebdige understands as subcultural style.[19] Defined as the reclaiming of an object or symbol and giving it new meaning, style is the defining feature of subcultural groups. It's an identity marker. It can be as simple as something like a safety pin or even Dr. Martens boots, but it can also be viewed as the embracing of stigma. It is taking the objects or gestures or passions that have been weaponised against you and embracing them. What a defiant act that is, the reinterpretation of stigma into style. Resistant, even. Reclaiming a label and proudly affirming its significance to your identity.

I didn't quite realise the positionality of this resistant stance until I fell down the rabbit hole into the awaiting arms of the Korean music group, BTS. It was like the pieces fell into place; the theory, the understanding, the experience all culminated into this one group. This one cultural object that I fell in love with. Because here were people talking about the things I believed in, the oppression of the lower classes, the trivialisation of female passion, the inequitable issues with neoliberal policy. These seven men, all around my age, all from different backgrounds were equally as frustrated as me. And it felt good. It felt good to know that my passions were legitimate. It felt good to be a part of a community that embraced the same ideals. And it felt good to be proud of my position as a fan as an act of resistance, because I wasn't alone. There were others, like me, occupying the same superpositions and conceptions of society as I did. Being a fan of BTS, being an ARMY was a political, resistant stance.[21] Being a fan of a group whose driving force is love *is* revolutionary.[22] And it was all the more better that my fan object happened to be occupying that defiant position alongside me.

Identity politics

But wasn't I still a fan? How was I to interrogate the space of this duality, this seemingly transgressive area I had yet to figure out?

Reconciling the trauma of working-class identity and the active participation in my own consumption patterns as a fan was something I had yet to investigate. Or rather, seeing my stigma as it relates to capitalism, rather than the patriarchy, was a realm I had yet to traverse. I feared myself falling into what Marx understands as a false consciousness,[23] but I also found divine pleasure in being a part of something, being a fan of something. It was who I was. It was what got me to this point. I couldn't give up what I was nurtured to believe. But at the same time, I couldn't go against the experiences of my upbringing that led me to align myself with more Socialist perspectives. I was at a crossroads, straddling a fence of my own making and I didn't want to fall to either side. I didn't want to leave one avenue behind while fully immersed in the other. Why couldn't I just be engaged in both?

I approached each space with hesitation. If I was buying BTS tour merch, I was a mindless consumer, blissfully naive in my own exploitation. If I called out Big Hit, BTS' entertainment company, for relying on the unpaid labour of fan translators, I was an "anti". In neither group was I "one of them". In neither space was I fully a part. Yet again I was faced with the overwhelming feeling of being not enough.

I had a choice to make: let the past repeat itself and live my life as someone I did not love for fear of defying my own ideology, or learn to live boldly, accepting myself for who I have always been and learn to love *being* that self. Looking back, it was an easy choice to make. But in those moments, where the intrusive thoughts refused to leave, the fear of letting not only those around me down but also myself almost swallowing me whole, it seemed almost impossible.

But of course I chose the latter.

Because each identity is made up of duality and it's the negotiation of both or all spaces that we occupy that makes us who we are. Understanding that and embracing that involves reflexivity, taking the time to look inward at those parts and see how they fit in relation to one another. This was a process I found myself undergoing, being understanding with the parts of me that were contradictory or stood in stark contrast to the other. It's what Drs. Christopher Germer and Kristen Neff call mindful self-compassion, where we take the time to understand ourselves through intentional gestures of empathy.[24] It's forgiveness through action, whether that's touch, writing, or meditation. Above all else, though, it's understanding. And understanding was what I needed.

Self-compassion became a ritual of sorts. It came in the evening meditations, daily writings. It came in the breathing techniques, the warding off of intrusive thoughts. And it evolved into love. Because compassion is love, isn't it? The root of empathy, the basis of care. All roads lead back to love. The meaning we give objects, the right for a just society, and the attachment towards a cultural icon — all of this finds its foundation laid upon the act of loving. And it was through these exercises that I understood that love, both of people and myself, was the boundary object between the two worlds.[25,26]

It was a mutual ground upon which both sides could agree; the construction of a Venn diagram out of the illusion of mutually exclusive circles.

Fan studies scholar Matt Hills understands that the fan experience is contradictory. Fans occupy both the space of consumption and production, agreeance and resistance.[9] It isn't black and white. Rather, it's in the grey areas where identity can be formed. And it's exactly those grey areas that stood as a meeting point upon which I could finally understand myself in relation to both contexts. And that's who I am; an obsessed, limerent fan who was also passionately anti-capitalist. Contradictory, sure, but me. And that's OK; I love *being* myself. I love that my heart seizes each time I watch the Jimin *Perfect Man* focus cam video on YouTube. I love that I cry each time I hear BTS' song *Mikrokosmos*, remembering the feeling of hearing it live with one of my best friends for the first time. I love being a fan. But I also love that I am steadfast in my beliefs for equity, for justice, and for a better society outside of the neoliberal capitalist system we are situated in. And why shouldn't I love who I am?

Outro: Speak yourself

Music and the working-class spirit have been long time lovers, intimately bound and interwoven in their construction of revolutionary constellations. I somehow forgot this for a while. I forgot that like the subcultures of the 1960s and 70s, cultural products like music could be the authentifying factor that solidified defiant identities.[1,19] I forgot that to be a revolutionary also meant to be *happy*. Embracing this identifying factor of stigma, of being a consumer in one regard and a pathologised fangirl in another, and reclaiming those titles through a form of style by wearing my fanship on my sleeve, was liberating. Ahmed talks about this in terms of love, how it, like shame, is also sticky, but the tackiness of the emotion instead binds us to one another.[13] Loving being myself through the act of loving how both passions align to make me who I am is sticky in the best sense because it binds me to my communities of equal taste, but it also adheres me to my roots.[14] To my values. To myself.

I cannot change the experiences of the past, nor would I want to because they make me who I am. If anything, those inform the choice I've made to *believe* in a better way for society. And it starts from loving myself and embracing that passion that fanship brings, a passion that has always been with me since the beginning. It's the same passion that helped me through the trauma of my childhood, the same passion that got me into grad school. Why should I deny that? Why *shouldn't* I love myself?

And isn't that resistance in itself? Isn't the grand proclamation of loving who I am and existing in this form within the oppressing confines of neoliberalist policy and late-stage capitalist systems absolutely defiant? As Marx claims, one of the goals of the capitalist system is to alienate us from our labour, from the fruits of our own production, and is coloured with exploitation from the top down.[2] This also extends into life itself, as we see with neoliberal ideology of competition, free market economies, the heavy emphasis on overarching productivity, and ultimately the individualisation of all things. It riddles our lives, permeates all spaces it can. It says you have to do this alone.

Fanship says otherwise. Fandom is community. It's egalitarian in nature, premised on collective feeling and connection. It can be shared values and opinions and taste.[14] It extends itself into our everyday, creating friendships, new modes of understanding, collective modes of creativity, and ultimately constructs safe spaces of identification.[20] It too riddles the lives of those who participate, bleeding out from the virtual and into the tangible. It says you *don't* have to do this alone. In fact, it screams out that you're *not* alone.

Like the rock 'n' roll my dad so admires specifically for its revolutionary spirit and anti-establishment sentiments, fandom is defiant. And it's beautiful. Though it took me some time to realise this, practising self-compassion and introspectively exploring where my identity sat within the paradigms of each realm, I came back to my roots. And I think that's why I love being who I am, love that I can explore both sides and see how each informs the other. And I hope that whether it's Freddie or Marx or maybe even both looking down on me, that they're proud.

References

1   Willis, P. E. (2014). *Profane culture*. Princeton University Press.
2   Ollman, B. (1977). *Alienation: Marx's conception of man in a capitalist society* (2nd ed.). Cambridge University Press.
3   Saad-Filho, A. (2002). *The value of Marx : Political economy for contemporary capitalism*. Routledge.
4   Sayers, S. (2014). *Marx and alienation: Essays on Hegelian themes*. Palgrave Macmillan.
5   Duffet, M. (2013). *Understanding fandom: An introduction to the study of media fan culture*. Bloomsbury Academic.
6   Lamerichs, N. (2018). *Productive fandom: Intermediality and affective reception in fan cultures*. Amsterdam University Press.
7   Sandvoss, C. (2014). "I ☒ IBIZA": Music, place and belonging. In M. Duffet (Ed.), *Popular music fandom: Identities, roles and practices* (pp. 115-145). Routledge.
8   Jenkins, H., Ito, M., & Boyd, D. (2016). *Participatory culture in a networked era: A conversation on youth, learning, commerce, and politics*. Polity Press.
9   Hills, M. (2002). *Fan cultures*. Routledge.
10 Jensen, J. (1992). Fandom as pathology: The consequences of characterization. In L.A. Lewis (Ed.), *The adoring audience: Fan culture and popular media* (pp. 9-29). Routledge.
11 Scott, S. (2019). *Fake geek girls: Fandom, gender, and the convergence culture industry*. NYU Press.
12 Poland, B. (2016). *Haters: Harassment, abuse, and violence online*. Potomac Books.
13 Ahmed, S. (2004). *The cultural politics of emotion*. Edinburgh University Press.

[14] Thornton, S. (1995). *Club cultures music, media and subcultural capital*. Polity Press.

[15] Eate, P. (2015). A New Dawn Breaks: Rewriting gender wrongs through Twilight fan fiction. In A. Trier-Bieniek (Ed.), *Fan girls and the media: Creating characters, consuming culture* (pp. 21-42). Rowman & Littlefield.

[16] Andrejevic, M. (2008). Watching television without pity. *Television & new media, 9*(1), 24-46.

[17] Bourdieu, P. (1984). *Distinction: A social critique of the judgement of taste*. Routledge.

[18] Goffman, E. (1963). *Stigma: Notes on the management of spoiled identity*. Penguin.

[19] Hebdige, D. (1981). *Subculture: The meaning of style*. Routledge.

[20] Woo, B. (2015). Nerds, geeks, gamers, and fans: Doing subculture on the edge of the mainstream. In A. Dhoest, S. Malliet, J. Haers, & B. Segaert (Eds.), *The borders of subculture: resistance and the mainstream* (1st ed., pp. 17-36). Routledge.

[21] Lee, J. (2019). *BTS and ARMY culture*. Communication Books.

[22] Eaglehawk, W. (2020). *Idol limerence: The art of loving BTS as phenomena*. Revolutionaries.

[23] Eyerman, R. (1981). False consciousness and ideology in Marxist theory. *Acta sociologica, 24*(1–2), 43–56.

[24] Germer, C., & Neff, K. (2019). Mindful self-compassion (MSC). In I. Ivtzan (Ed.), *The handbook of mindfulness-based programs: Every established intervention, from medicine to education* (pp. 357-367). Routledge.

[25] Star, S., & Griesemer, J. (1989). Institutional ecology, 'Translations' and boundary objects: amateurs and

professionals in Berkeley's Museum of Vertebrate Zoology, 1907-39. *Social studies of science, 19*(3), 387-420.

[26] Fox, N. J. (2011). Boundary objects, social meanings and the success of new technologies. *Sociology, 45*(1), 70–85.

THE BROKEN VASE THEORY

Gabrielle S. Punzalan

Intro: "What will you do with the broken shards?"

Although I do not completely love myself, there was a time when I completely hated myself. It should be alarming how one extreme seems unattainable while the other comes to me so naturally. Yet this disposition is common in today's society, with rates of depression, anxiety, and suicide of young people being higher than rates of previous generations.[1] The time I completely hated myself may also be considered to be the plot of a standard, coming-of-age film: the family is evicted, the character has to transfer to a new school, the character struggles spiritually when the family church closes but eventually goes on a life-changing adventure that will help them discover their identity. This is usually what is expected to happen, and in 2018, I restlessly awaited my character arc once my picture-perfect downfall played out. However, the reality is harsher and more cruel than the romanticised coming of age depicted in Hollywood.

Rather than the big picture, I witnessed the gritty details that aren't portrayed on screens. Three years ago when I was 15, my family got evicted from my childhood home and we had to close the family church where I dedicated most of my time, spiralling me into a conflict of faith. I transferred in the middle of the school year when people had already established their friendships, and the friendships I did have suddenly were no longer in my life. Although these are standard, stereotypical problems that many young people face at a glance, these were the catalyst for bigger worries and questions in my life.

All these elements that made up my status quo were taken from me, stripping my identity bare, and leaving me confused as to who I was as an individual. Rather than the character growth I expected in the face of my circumstances, I became a straggler trying to find where I belonged in this new setting. I was used to relying on external validation in order to maintain stability. The reason why I hated myself was because without these external outlets that built my identity, I could no longer hide my insecurities. I could no longer cover up the complexities in my identity that I had tried to reject. My authentic self that I had suppressed, in favour of a persona to gain acceptance, was starting to show after years of wearing a mask.

It was during this period of self-hatred in my sophomore year that I was introduced to the shattered vase metaphor — often coined the 'broken vase theory' — which changed my perspective on the world and of myself. The theory is used in psychology to "explain the possible ways in which people react to negative (even traumatic) experiences."[2] I believe the broken vase theory can be explored as not only a metaphor for dealing with negative experiences but as a ritual of self-care — an activity done deliberately to maintain well-being.[3] Applying the metaphor to life is an activity that when continuously done, "opens space for us to facilitate changes in other parts of our lives".[3]

Self-love for me is being able to let go of my insecurities and to embrace my complexities rather than rejecting them. In order to address my complexities at home and within, I needed to find a way to love myself and find self-acceptance instead of searching for love externally. What resonated with me may resonate with whoever reads this, so here I am laying out the broken shards of my youth with the knowledge that mobilising towards self-love can be as simple as being asked: *"What will you do with the broken shards?"*

Part I: My shattered status quo

Mental health has always been a taboo topic in my immigrant, conservative, and religious household.[4] As a result, I've learnt to internalise all my feelings. Thus, I grew up feeling alone in assessing why my complexities made me feel like an outsider. My status quo was formed upon the instability of my cultural heritage, spiritual beliefs, and the downfalls of being a middle child. I was trying to juggle all of these in order to make a stable identity for myself, and my desperation for a sense of belonging led to me constantly searching for the love externally. However, what I have learnt is that external validation can never fully satisfy the yearning for self acceptance.

My parents immigrated to America as teenagers after being raised in the Philippines during the dictatorship of Ferdinand Marcos. I don't know much about my cultural heritage besides what I've been exposed to through my parents. When I was younger, I even tried to reject my culture altogether. My parents grew up in their native country surrounded by peers who all shared the same culture. As a young, first-generation American, I only understood that my culture at home was not the norm elsewhere when everyone would stare at me eating my food.

Many of the questions would be along this line "what are you eating? It looks gross...". It was asked more to show disgust rather than genuine interest in learning what was different about my Filipino culture. As a child hearing these remarks, I could only connect my culture to feeling lesser than. The stares and the remarks... It was like every bite I took from the Filipino savoury pork, hot bun (called 'siopao') my mom packed was being scrutinised. However, when I started to bring Lunchables — a brand of standard, American meal and snack combos — to school, it was something my classmates were familiar with and accepted, and in turn started to accept me as well. I understood from a young age that conforming to the dominant American culture in school meant not sticking out like a sore thumb. The effects of this acculturation, however, meant "internalising the experiences of feeling lesser than" in a phenomenon termed as the 'immigrant paradox' in which first-generation, "US-born youth are more likely to experience higher rates of mental health problems than youth who immigrated from a foreign country."[4] First-generation Americans tend to harbour resentment for their cultural identity, as compared to their immigrant parents, due to the systemic racism and the pressure to fit in.[4]

There were also moments of feeling lesser than within my own household. I come from a family of all daughters, me being the middle child. Though there's no doubt in my mind that our parents love us all equally (and they made a point of making sure we knew), I found myself seeking to validate my place in this family. Family roles and dynamics meant not having the expectations of being the eldest daughter, but no longer having the attention of being the youngest. Birth order is like being born into a competition where you're the only one actively competing, and somehow you're still losing. Being a middle child feels like that.

I abruptly went from being a B-C average grade student to receiving honour roll, working hard to get the grades I knew would make my parents proud. I made it my goal to score higher than my big sister on the required Scholastic Aptitude Test (SAT) if it meant having approval from our parents that she didn't have. I had different obsessions from random film trivia to musical theatre, fandoms to have a group to belong with, and hyper-fixations on things that would make me stand out from the sandwich I'm smushed in. Learning how to solve a Rubik's Cube in order to impress my family may seem like overkill, but I assure you it's something I did — and I can solve it in a minute flat. This case of middle child syndrome contributed to my fear of neglect that was reinforced by the stress of fitting in within school and society.[5] Insecure attachments to my parents came from the constant need to compensate, rather than learning how to cope.

People pleasing usually stems from a childhood of trying to please parents to "maintain connection and closeness" with them, such as the effects of middle child syndrome.[6] Combine that with the immigrant paradox and you have a psychological nightmare. The byproduct from feeling like an outsider on all these fronts for me was people pleasing. I resorted to people pleasing at some point to solve all my problems. I didn't even realise I started to have a "strong desire for approval and external validation".[7] It can be seen when I begged my parents for Lunchables or when I sought validation from my parents. I managed other people's emotions and never my own, contributing to my growing pile of unresolved trauma. My people-pleasing tendencies soon branched out into other behavioural patterns.

Growing up in church and descending from two generations of pastors, it is hard to distinguish the fine line that separates religion from my identity since it had *become* my identity — or rather, the 'persona' I showed around my family. 'Persona' is defined as the "personality that an individual projects to others, as differentiated from the authentic self."[8] I was active in church, serving in the praise and worship team and attending youth group weekly, but this persona was more to meet the expectations associated with the beliefs I was raised on. Religion became another outlet for external validation from my pastor father, my religious mother, and my devout grandparents. I used religion to hide that my authentic self was based on the approval of others rather than from reverence in Christ. I believed in the existence of God, but external validation was the sovereign power in my life.

I allowed my complexities to become my insecurities. The combined byproducts that came from my conservative, immigrant household have resulted in a poorly patched up state of limbo. It wouldn't matter that I developed insecure attachments to my parents and started seeking validation from superficial achievements. I told myself that life will go smoothly as long as I conform to my surroundings.

This was the status quo I knew, but even that facade of stability was proven to be weak when I was unprepared to face the trauma of sophomore year. My school, my church, my friends, my home — all the constants in my life that I relied on to keep the status quo were taken from me and I had no control over it. The first day at my new school was as horrible as I expected it to be. Coming from a metropolitan school, it was a culture shock to pass all the cows grazing in the large pasture; I went from downtown to the back roads of a cow farm. The first sign of trouble was a local news truck that was parked in front of the school. Though I initially was confused on what news could possibly be covered at a school in the middle of nowhere, I later found out it had something to do with a viral video that involved a school cheerleader and a racial slur.

Already off to a terrible start.

I tried to hold myself together with false optimism: excited to make new friends, ecstatic to start classes, ready to face the day. I was lying to myself. Even my false optimism couldn't sugar coat the tribulations of the day. It didn't help that not a single person approached me to greet me or even acknowledge me as the new student. I started to get stares again; the stares that let a person know they're different, that they're less than. I felt alienated by my peers — estranged from everything going on around me and just going through the motions.[9] No one seemed to relate with me and since my family had already settled in, I was the only one not adapting. Like I was being left behind.

The status quo shattered despite doing everything in my power to make sure it wouldn't. Questioning the status quo felt unimaginable but having it shatter meant starting from square one with a clean slate and no instructions. When I started to feel lost and have thoughts that contradicted the beliefs I was raised on, I questioned everything I had come to know.

Did God abandon me? What did I do to deserve this? Why are all these bad things happening to me?

Eventually, everything fell apart.

I texted a crisis line that night, and I poured out all the feelings I had internalised for as long as I could remember. They told me to write my feelings down and I ended up writing a suicide note: a cry for help. As a last resort, I showed it to my parents, which ultimately pushed them to bring me to a therapist.

Part II: Creating something new

I attended my appointment at My Secret Garden Counselling Center early on a Monday morning. The therapist, who specialised in helping teens through play therapy, asked me to draw a vase however I wanted. When I sketched one on paper, I added flowers and coloured them with the Crayola colouring markers provided; my inner child was released. When I finished, she complimented my toddler-style art and asked how I feel about my vase. I told her that despite my lack of artistic ability and using up 20 minutes of our one-hour appointment, I was very proud of my drawing.

"You probably saw this coming," she warned me before ripping apart my masterpiece, showing that my vase is shattered. The strips of paper were shards of my broken vase. She then asked me a vital question: *"What will you do with the broken shards?"* She told me that I had these options: I could do nothing. I could sweep it under the rug, but how long would I go on not dealing with the remains? What would I resolve by keeping a broken vase? I could try putting the pieces back together, but the vase would never be the same, barely held together by tape or glue. However, she offered me a different option of accepting that the breakage is part of the process of becoming stronger. Instead of trying to restore the vase to its former glory, the broken shards can now become something more resilient. This is the broken vase theory as I was taught: a vase on the ledge of a table is a metaphor for the assumptive world. Adversity is the equivalent to knocking the vase over the ledge to shatter on the floor. The different ways people may deal with the broken shards describes how people may deal differently with experiencing trauma.

The broken vase theory was developed from renowned child psychiatrist Jean Piaget's theories of cognitive development that account for how humans adapt through the process of assimilation and accommodation.[10] Assimilation is defined as "making new information fit in with an existing understanding of the world,"[11] whereas accommodation is "modifying old ideas or even replacing them based on new information."[11] Dr. Stephen Joseph explains that the theory helps people to find the "right balance of assimilation and accommodation" for themselves.[9]

We can see challenges as opportunities to learn more about ourselves rather than as hindrances. This will make us more perceptible to post-traumatic growth, which "involves the rebuilding of the shattered assumptive world."[10] During this process we can make ourselves more resilient by taking the time to reevaluate our capabilities (which may be greater than we had known), our values (what we put importance on may have changed), and our boundaries (which may not have been healthily established before). Studies by Dr. Richard Tedeschi and Dr. Lawrence Calhoun show that people who experience post-traumatic growth "develop a new appreciation of life, newfound personal strength, see an improvement in their relationships, see new possibilities in life, and undergo spiritual changes."[12] In my case, the broken vase theory was also my first step towards choosing self-acceptance and self-love, and eventually breaking from my people-pleaser mindset. Being more open to change, I embarked on a conceptual journey of trying to piece myself back together to make the 'new' me — a colourful mosaic created from my complexities.

I learned that it is up to me to actively work towards self-awareness and to choose to be happy. Strength comes through managing life's challenges after all. Dorothy Ratsuny, a psychotherapist, writes that "your mental well-being is based on what you are able to do for yourself."[13] These words ring true for everyone, including me. Once

I understood that the answer to acceptance lay with me, I started to undo what I had internalised due to my complexities. I could start regaining my confidence through actions of self-love and care. As a people pleaser, the most monumental change I could do was to set healthy, personal boundaries that weren't in place earlier. This includes learning to be "more assertive and more self-protective" compared to when I would usually take on the burdens of other people's expectations and judgements.[7] I'm now understanding what I am and am not accountable for, and that it is not my responsibility to be accountable for others' responsibilities.

By practising saying no, I am nursing my lowered self-regard that comes from being a people pleaser. When my first instinct is to apologise, even if it's not my fault or when someone mocks me for my interests — it is up to me to stand up for myself and to resist pressure. People pleasing is not generosity; to stand my ground when under pressure is to become more resilient than my prior fragility.

Self-love is a choice and by associating and assimilating you are reminding yourself to "decide how you want to feel and to mobilize yourself towards what will allow you to feel content, peaceful and happy — now."[13] Life will always have trials that are inevitable, but it is how we persevere through them that matters. Through a balance of assimilation and association, I am navigating through whatever life throws at me. I am building up my confidence and self-trust, building myself anew.

Outro: "All of this is leading up to something better."

At the time of writing this — and perhaps even after — I still am learning ways to love myself. Writing this essay in itself is a radical act of self-love: A 19-year-old aspiring writer who is afraid to share her work decided to submit it to a call for submissions and share her story with readers. I'm still struggling with the same inner battles and the same doubts I've had from years ago, but what encouraged me to write about self-love despite all of this is that I am only human like everyone else; these struggles are universal and not limited to only me. During a time when self-esteem is especially challenged, advocating self-love and self-care is more critical now than ever before.[14]

When I first started writing this essay, I was leaning back in a cushioned chair with my laptop and a bottle of tea on the table while listening to music and enjoying the sparkling lights on the horizon of the Vegas Strip from my hotel room on the 12th floor. Being able to witness these luxuries reminds me of how far I've come from that shy, lost sophomore girl who had just transferred. Although I do not completely love myself, I am higher than where I was three years ago — the 12th floor is much higher than rock bottom. At the time of writing, the traumatic year of 2020 is finally coming to its conclusion and I am reminded of the theory once again. This time I am asking myself what I will take from the aftermath of 2020 and how I will utilise it moving forward.

BTS, a Korean music group who are also regarded as outsiders within the music industry, have always been advocates of self-love and have never changed who they are as artists to conform to American standards. Seeing such authentic Asian representation inspires me to embrace who I am as well. Their lyrics act as affirmations in letting go of my insecurities, especially in BTS' song 2! 3! (둘! 셋!) lyrics: "Let's only walk on the flower road. I can't say such words".[15]

This metaphor of the flower path translates to "let's walk on a road filled with happiness and success together".[16] However, in the song, BTS member RM says that he can't promise us this, that things will not always be good but we can still hope that things will get better from now on.[15] BTS speak from personal experience about how the path of happiness, success, and self-acceptance is a hard-fought journey. Walking this path will not always be easy and will be riddled with hardships, but my therapist reminded me during my appointment that "all of this is leading up to something better".

Many will wonder as much as I have: "Why are all these bad things happening to me?" We will wonder why life can't be like a flower path where everything is perfect and always goes smoothly. As someone who has asked myself, the universe, and God for the answers to these questions, I am writing with all my heart, after rising from rock bottom and seeing the breathtaking view from the 12th floor, that people become stronger and more resilient by managing through life's challenges. In a similar way, BTS' rise to fame was not an easy path. RM uses the flower path metaphor to remind listeners that the journey to self-love will be rough, but rewarding. The hardships, the friends we make and sometimes lose, the days you want to just give up, the nights when you're drowning in your own thoughts: all of this is leading up to something greater. That greater thing could be yourself.

References

1   Duffy, M., Twenge, J., & Joiner, T. (2019). *Trends in mood and anxiety symptoms and suicide-related outcomes among U.S. undergraduates, 2007–2018: Evidence from two national surveys. Journal of adolescent health, 65*(5), 590-598.

2   Raghavendra, K. (2020, August 1). *The shattered vase theory.* https://medium.com/a-good-life/the-shattered-vase-theory-eb040f213ec1.

3   Bartz, J. (2019, June 17). *The importance of ritual in self-care.* https://www.mindful.nyc/blog/2019/6/17/the-importance-of-ritual-in-self-care.

4   Borge, J. (2020, July 27). *How being a first-generation American affected my mental health.* https://www.health.com/mind-body/first-generation-american-mental-health-immigrant-paradox

5   Werner, C. (2020, November 10). *Birth order and personality: The science behind middle child syndrome.* https://www.healthline.com/health/mental-health/middle-child-syndrome.

6   Stoneson, A. (2013, April). *What makes a people-pleaser.* https://labyrinthhealing.com/blog/what-makes-a-people-pleaser.

7   Gattuso, R. (2018, August 9). *How does people pleasing negatively affect your mental health?* https://www.talkspace.com/blog/people-pleasing-negatively-affect-mental-health/.

8   Britannica, T. Editors of Encyclopaedia (2008, April 4). *Persona.* https://www.britannica.com/science/persona-psychology.

9   Barclay, R. (2018, February 8). *Alienation.* https://www.healthline.com/health/alienation.

10   Joseph, S. (2012, May 21). *The metaphor of the shattered vase.* https://www.psychologytoday.com/us/blog/what-doesnt-kill-us/201205/the-metaphor-the-shattered-vase.

11 Cherry, K. (2020, May 15). *The importance of assimilation in adaptation.* https://www.verywellmind.com/what-is-assimilation-2794821.

12 Luna, K. (Host). (2019, December). *Transformation after trauma (96).* https://www.apa.org/research/action/speaking-of-psychology/transformation-trauma.

13 Ratusny, D. (2020, May 13). *Radical love and self-acceptance in a time of crisis, anxiety, depression, and loneliness.* https://thriveglobal.com/stories/radical-love-and-self-acceptance-in-a-time-of-crisis-anxiety-depression-and-loneliness/.

14 Czeisler, M., Lane, R., Petrosky, E., Wiley, J., Christensen, A., Njai, R., Weaver, M., Robbins, R., Facer-Childs, E., Barger, L., Czeisler, C., Howard, M., & Rajaratnam, S. (2020, August 14). *Mental health, substance use, and suicidal ideation during the COVID-19 pandemic — United States, June 24–30, 2020.* Morbidity and mortality weekly report. http://dx.doi.org/10.15585/mmwr.mm6932a1.

15 BTS. (2016). 둘! 셋! (그래도 좋은 날이 더 많기를) [Two! Three! (Still wishing there will be more good days)] [Song]. On *You never walk alone.* Big Hit Entertainment; Doolset. (2018). 둘! 셋! Two! Three! [Translation]. https://doolsetbangtan.wordpress.com/2018/06/01/two-three/.

16 Choi, M. (2018, July 17). Kpop slang: 꽃길만 걷자 (Let's walk along the road with flowers). https://medium.com/story-of-eggbun-education/kpop-slang-%EA%BD%83%EA%B8%B8%EB%A7%8C-%EA%B1%B7%EC%9E%90-lets-walk-along-the-road-with-flowers-1c3e2ec2c22e.

DOSES OF SELF-ACCEPTANCE

Rashifa Aljunied

Invisible illness and stigma

Loving myself has been hard when my body cannot cope with the things I want to do in my everyday life. I am vulnerable to the change in temperature, even though I live in a tropical country. I have the same diet every day and yet my body has different allergies every single day. I have no diagnosis and thus, my pain has no name. So do I love myself? Yes and no, depending on how I am feeling. Sometimes I feel guilty for being happy when my body is in excruciating pain. I have come to realise that even when I am sick, I can still manage to be genuinely happy and fulfilled, and hence love myself. Loving myself, inside and out, means that I am content with how I am, no matter the circumstances.

I discovered BTS during the pandemic, and their songs gave me new understanding into how people can be uplifted by their love yourself lyrics, musicality, and performances. In *Dis-ease* there's the phrase that goes "even your mind needs a vacation."[1] Your mind is the ultimate controller of your body. The song gives me hope that every illness, including mine, has its own medicine, once I decide to face it. The feeling of hopelessness, and then facing it with positivity can be a healing process. The lyrics of BTS were like the mirror of my own thoughts. They gave me a reason to write what I was feeling as BTS are not afraid to share stories about bullying, depression, the inevitable struggles of youth, pursuit of happiness, and fitting oneself into the ideals of society and temptation.

Self-love is hard work. It took me a year's worth of therapy to get to the level of self-appreciation that I now am experiencing. I have a sense of passion in writing and I put hard work into everything I do. Self-hate still comes along when my body fails to keep with me. I now realise that I cannot be perfect whenever I want to and I need to give my body the time that it needs to rest and heal. I believe a lot of people misunderstand how a person with a chronic illness can love themselves. This is because they seem to think that a person who is ill would be depressed or at least sad all the time. Depression can be part of chronic illness but it does not have to be so. At the same time I am learning to love myself when I feel depressed and when I am in pain. Having an illness may be a burden, but I cannot let it be a weight that holds me down forever. Then stigma came along.

Living with an invisible illness means that I live with stigma. Stigma engulfs my life. People don't understand me, and I don't understand my conditions and symptoms myself. It creates the perspective that I'm 'faking' my illness, usually for attention. I do not have a visible, physical disability. Due to the invisible nature of my condition I am stigmatised even by my own peers, family, and doctors. Stigma involves exclusion and devaluation of people, including people with mental illness and chronic conditions, by using negative stereotypes.[2]

According to Goffman, negative labelling and stereotyping of people can create feelings of shame and self-hate.[3] For me, it showed as a disparity between what I share online about myself compared to how people perceive me in reality and my actual social identity. The little habits that I have, such as hiding my condition, and suppressing my anxiety (by holding my breath so I don't sound anxious) are the by-product of being stigmatised. These habits are my coping mechanism. It's the self-identity I keep in private. This further perpetuates stigma by others and creates self-stigma by my own actions. Self-stigma is where self-hatred can creep in. We often want to find someone to blame, but at the end of the day, we end up feeling guilty. I often find myself saying sorry unconsciously, being afraid that I would be a hassle to someone.

Anxiety, guilt, and shame are not the only feelings that come with my experience of stigma. There is also a feeling of unfairness underneath my effort to love myself with an invisible illness. Stigma is a form of discrimination which can have negative impacts on people. Discrimination involves treating people unfairly by stereotyping them in negative ways.

The process of stereotyping, according to sociologists Link and Phelan, has four steps: labelling of the differences the person has; identifying the differences; separating what they don't understand as different, and lastly; the process of discriminating against the person.[4]

Ableism or able-bodiedness is discrimination that happens when able-bodied people treat your invisible illness, invisibly, like literally not acknowledging the fact that you do have a chronic condition.[5] Ableism occurs when disabilities are treated as a type of deviance from the desired social norm of able-bodiedness.[5] You are taken as disposable and less than human, seen as socially devalued and low in competence.[6]

Being stigmatised for a medical condition has impacted me psychologically and emotionally. As surprised as I am with how people with invisible illness are stigmatised, I never expected the health care system to be as biased against me as they were. When seeking medical help to get a diagnosis I found doctors were cold and matter of fact. They didn't seem to have any care for me and what a lack of diagnosis means. Through disempowering experiences such as this, I have had to work hard to appreciate and love myself. I realise I have to be my own mental wellbeing and physical health advocate.

Validation and self-acceptance

Life without a concrete diagnosis is incredibly frustrating. I firmly believe that no matter how stressed I am, pain is the body's alert device, an adaptive reaction to potential danger. If you think you're at risk, the brain can make you feel uncomfortable. The frustration of being in pain is extremely toxic to me. According to Encandela, "there are essentially two continuums of pain [and] suffering: one comprises the degree of mental pain and the other of the severity of physical pain."[7] These strands interact in a single experience of pain such that our responses to either type of pain tend to be identical.[8] This makes sense because when I'm in pain I'm angry and when I'm angry I'm in pain.

I struggled for a long time with imposter syndrome, of feeling fake, and the lack of validation about my illness from others. This all changed when I found an online community that I can lean on. It has given me strength that I never expected after being in pain for so long. NEISVoid is a hashtag community on Twitter which has been a pillar of strength for me for months now. Its members are other people with chronic conditions who continuously share encouragement and words of affirmation, and also tips on daily life activities. Validation of pain-related thoughts and feelings can contribute to a decrease in negative effects.[9] I am more and more able to face my illness, face on.

I'm still on a journey of self-discovery and trying to rise up to the challenges of living life with an invisible illness. I have come to understand that my 'curse,' or pain that I face daily, was given to me for a reason. It must be. So, no matter what, I will do whatever it takes and in my power, to love myself. I also want to encourage other people with invisible illnesses to resist negative labels about them, in the same way I was helped by the online community. I know from my own experience that it is so easy to feel alone, defeated, and so hard to get back up. It isn't as hard when you have a community of like-minded people supporting you to rise up.

Healing through music, dance, and writing

I believe BTS' music has been central to my healing and learning to love myself. I'm letting BTS hold my hands when others aren't around. Being emotionally self-reliant is great, and with BTS willing to be by my side, I feel invincible. "Though I'd get tired and hurt sometimes, it's okay because I'm next to you. Because, you and I, if we're together, we can smile".[10] BTS' words are affirmation to me. I let myself be affirmed by young men from South Korea, and I'm fine by that. Inspired by BTS, I often find myself dancing freely in my room to their music. It has helped me release a lot of the pent-up frustration and anger that I have. I let my body move to the rhythm however I want to, not focusing on how I look.

Their lyrics have opened me up to the power of spoken poetry which has helped me in expressing thoughts that I can't explain in my own words. In China, people believe that the performing arts have a restorative and protective effect on both body and soul.[11] Shen Yun Performing Arts may be the most unforgettable and convincing creative example of art that is at the same time, since it has a score, providing the potential of being both soothing and encouraging. Many who have watched Shen Yun report that a tranquil and joyful energy that emerges from his shows talk to them after a showing.[11] I imagine that feeling when I am dancing in my room listening to BTS.

I have also discovered the power of writing. Transforming my emotions into words has lessened the burden that I put on my shoulders. It helps prove to me that my feelings are valid. I can have an overwhelming mix of thoughts in my head, and sometimes it is definitely hard to grasp those thoughts to make real meaning out of them. Any piece of writing is an expression of your own unique personal voice. It stands for us while we are not here. It lets people know about our capacity, goals, the extent of our skills, and our plans for the future. According to Laura A. King, writing about life aspirations is less distressing than writing about trauma, and it is linked to a substantial improvement in subjective wellbeing.[12] No one can do it for me. So when I write, I am able to portray my ambiguous anxiety into an organised form of art, which is in words, and then a paragraph and then potentially an article. I commit to my life aspirations by writing through my pain.

Self-acceptance: The ideal medication

At times the reality of the pain that I was having every day seems to fade away and I question myself whether I was just making everything up. The worst is when people close to you question your condition, and when they think it's time to stop meeting the doctors when you're still full of hope. Every night I have a bitter smell on my fingers after taking my medication and I hate it. I also hate the bitter taste in my mouth before I sleep. But I need to get better. I need to have an open mind if I do actually want to get better. It gets worse, before it gets better. My friends and family are extremely hopeful. I can't tell them I won't get better, that's too cruel. So I tell them it's a long road ahead, please be prepared to hold my hands if I get too tired. I tell them I'll do the same for them as well. With a chronic condition, you will spend a lot of time managing other people's emotions.

Years go by incredibly slow, but days go by so fast. Life in my twenties is extremely exciting and exhilarating. But as fun as life is right now, there are so many things that have brought me down. It's incredibly easy to feel defeated. And it's hard to get back up. This is how I feel right now. I'm standing on the beach, my foot sinks in the sand while shallow water comes up to my ankle. A wave is coming, and it splashes me until I fall down. But I have to get back up again. With the waves crashing over and over again, I'm getting back up again and again. The waves overwhelm me, deafening my ears as I tumble backwards. I am constantly being thrown into situations that I am uncomfortable with, challenges in life that I was not taught how to handle. But I am constantly learning.

My pain, anxiety, and depression will always shadow me, but I will not let them drag me down. I will stand with grace, knowing that there are better days to come with no promised tomorrows. Getting hurt could be from an illness, but it could also be the incidents in our everyday life. Good things will come when times are rough, and I will continue to walk at my own pace now understanding that self-acceptance is the ideal medication.

References

[1]   BTS. (2020). Dis-ease (병) [Song]. On *Be*. Big Hit Entertainment.; Doolset. (2020) 병 (Dis-ease) [Translation]. https://doolsetbangtan.wordpress.com/2020/11/20/dis-ease/

[2]   Goffman E. (1963) *Stigma: Notes on the management of spoiled identity.* Penguin.

[3]   Goffman, E. (1959). *The presentation of self in everyday life.* Doubleday.

[4]   Link, B. G., Struening, E. L., Rahav, M., Phelan, J. C., & Nuttbrock, L. (1997). On stigma and its consequences: evidence from a longitudinal study of men with dual diagnoses of mental illness and substance abuse. *Journal of health and social behavior*, 177-190.

[5]   Campbell, F. (2009). *Contours of ableism: The production of disability and abledness.* Springer.

[6]   Fricker, M. (2007). *Epistemic injustice: Power and the ethics of knowing.* Oxford University Press.

[7]   Encandela, J. (1993). Social science and the study of pain since Zborowski: A need for a new agenda. *Social science & medicine*, *36*(6), 783-791.

[8]   Taylor, S. S., Davis, M. C., Yeung, E. W., Zautra, A. J., & Tennen, H. A. (2017). Relations between adaptive and maladaptive pain cognitions and within-day pain exacerbations in individuals with fibromyalgia. *Journal of behavioral medicine*, *40*(3), 458-467.

[9]   Kool, W., McGuire, J. T., Rosen, Z. B., & Botvinick, M. M. (2010). Decision making and the avoidance of cognitive demand. *Journal of experimental psychology: general*, *139*(4), 665.

10   BTS. (2017). A Supplementary Story: You never walk alone
[Song]. On *You never walk alone*. Big Hit Entertainment.;
Doolset. (2018). *A supplementary story: You never walk
alone* [Translation]. https://doolsetbangtan.wordpress.
com/2018/06/01/a-supplementary-story-you-never-walk-alone/

11   Yang, J. (2012, December 4). *The healing power of performing
arts*. https://www.huffpost.com/entry/arts-health_b_1421645.

12   King, L. A. (2001). The health benefits of writing about life
goals. *Personality and social psychology bulletin*, 27(7), 798–807.

(RE)WRITING MY LIFE AS AN ASIAN AMERICAN: SHATTERING ILLUSORY TRUTH ONE WORD AT A TIME

Devin Barney

I lie supine on my bed. Save for the erratic rising and falling of my chest, I am completely still. Despite the stillness, I can feel my heart thunderously drumming, a veritable percussive ensemble exploiting my sternum for rehearsal space. With immense effort, as if waving my own conductor's baton, I attempt to impose a new, singular rhythm on my body: Breathe in, 2, 3, 4; Hold, 2, 3, 4; Breathe out, 2, 3, 4. I muster all the mindfulness intention that I can and focus on my breath. But a thorny thought pierces my concentration: *You're failing at this; you're a failure.* I wave it away and try again: Breathe In, 2, 3, 4; Hold 2, 3— *You suck. You can't even breathe right.* Once more: Breathe In, 2, 3— *Why do you bother trying? You're worthless.*

I give up on the breath control and try distracting myself instead. I want to reach for my laptop to play a film but my body has yet to yield me meaningful, volitional control. I settle for opening my eyes and peering up at my ceiling. Cold, blue-grey tendrils of light creep their way beyond my blackout curtains, dimly illuminating even colder, greyer ceiling tiles. I try to count them: 1, 2, 3, 4, 5— *Wait, I think I counted that one twice. 1, 2, 3, 4— Seriously!? You can't even count tiles? You're such a waste of space.* A few more trials of counting tiles and my mental space has devolved into an all-out battlefield, and there's nothing I can do to protect myself from volley after volley of assault.

Unable. Undesirable. Unworthy. Unloved. Ugly. Useless. Weak. Burdensome. Lazy. Selfish. Trash. Freak. Imposter. Embarrassment. Leech. Stupid. Cancer. Depressing. Lost cause. Overly sensitive. Bad son. Bad friend. Bad student. Bad roommate. Never enough.

Instinctively, I cower into a rigid ball to defend myself against the onslaught of these sentiments. But it is all for naught because these thoughts burn so hotly in my mind, it is as if my very flesh were being branded with these words. Immeasurable time passes as I lie in wait for the fiery pain to cease. When it does, my frozen body can no longer hold its tension and collapses further into my mattress. With the ebb of negative self-thought follows the flow of self-preservation doing its best to nudge me into action: *Hydrate. Eat. Relieve yourself.* This time I am able to comply with the call and gingerly remove myself from the bed to trudge to my bathroom. A mirror runs the length of the far wall of my bathroom, so when I stumble inside, I am forced to see my still-glowing brands. I avert my eyes immediately. I despise what I see.

I'm reminded of RM's lamentation of his own *Reflection* (2016) "나는 내가 너무너무 미워" [I really, really hate myself] and his closing refrain "I wish I could love myself".[1] In lucid moments, I find myself wishing for the same thing. The ethos of BTS points to self-love, not only as an achievable possibility, but almost a moral imperative; yet the roadmap towards self-love for me is hazy. How do I learn to love myself when I hate myself so deeply?

Like many ARMY, BTS found me when I needed them most. I was introduced to BTS by a dear friend in July 2019, during a brief layover I had enroute home from an academic conference. As undergraduates, she and I had shared in many artistic endeavours — I was a vocalist, dancer, actor, theatrical director, and theatrical designer; she was a poet, playwright, painter, scenic designer, and one of the most incredible storytellers I have had the pleasure of knowing. But I had all but stopped my participation and engagement in the arts for a few years to pursue science — a PhD in psychology. Knowing my art world hiatus had greyed my world, she sat me down and presented a carefully curated, comprehensive survey of BTS' work. She imbued this introduction with as much of her love of BTS as she could. It was truly infectious. While I didn't initially understand their lyrics, I was immediately mesmerised by their voices, performance quality, and aesthetic. I left Los Angeles with technicolour vision and a renewed sense of love for what art could be and do. I had no idea then just how powerfully impactful BTS would be for me.

Fast forward to 2020 and the beginning of the COVID-19 pandemic — days like the one I described above were common for me. In an effort to maintain physical distance and slow the spread of the virus, I, like many others, began working remotely from home and remained in physical quarantine as much as possible.[2] All the activities, spaces, and people I used to distract myself were completely gone. Living with myself became increasingly unbearable because I had little to buffer myself from my thoughts. BTS became my one escape, my one solace, my one support. I turned to their music, their performances, their variety shows, their travel series, and their live vlogs. Through BTS I was able to inhabit their joy, their sadness, their strife, their achievement, and find valuable moments of connection, empathy, and most importantly relief from my own pain, emptiness, and loneliness. But with every replay of *Reflection*, *Epiphany*, or *Answer: Love Myself* or every rewatch of their speech at the UN, I was compelled to acknowledge that the very root of my ills, my self-hatred, was being largely ignored. How do I learn to love myself when I hate myself so deeply?

Facing another mounting mental health crisis, I was encouraged by a friend to reach out for professional help. Energised by BTS and a sense of hope for better days, I started seeing a therapist on a regular basis. It was during these sessions that I gained an immensely powerful insight that would illuminate my path forward toward self-love. During one of our conversations, my therapist mentioned off-handedly that sometimes we develop a poor relationship with ourselves because we learn untrue things about ourselves from repetition of negative messages. Being the curious psychology academic that I am, I searched to see if such ideas were validated by psychological science. Indeed — science called it the 'illusory truth effect.'

Illusory truths are assertions we come to falsely believe are true. The illusory truth effect is the means by which we come to believe these falsehoods. Through repeated exposure to an idea, we forget how or where or when we might have heard that idea, and it becomes increasingly familiar to us and so we assume that it must be true.[3] Repetition of an idea leads to an increased sense of familiarity and familiarity leads to greater processing fluency which compels us to lean into an intuition that the notion is true.[4] This mental shortcut whereby familiarity is synonymous with truth value was at one point adaptive — it helped us to make quicker and better decisions for ourselves. However, in an age of fake news and social stigma wherein our social environment is replete with untrue assertions, this mental shortcut becomes a double-edged sword. We may indeed process this information more quickly, but we do so internalising things that may come to hurt us. Believing in fake news can mislead us to harmful decisions. Believing in social stigma can mislead us to harmful thoughts and self-conceptions.

Self-hate and self-love share a common foundation of care and passion; you have to care enough about yourself to hate or love yourself. Through this acknowledgement in their work and in their daily lives, BTS illuminates for me a destination wherein it is indeed possible to repair a relationship with yourself and transform that relation from one of self-hate to self-love. Psychological science is a torch for me to shine onto the path towards that destination wherein I can see the steps I need to take to make that happen. I have been fooled into believing falsehoods about myself as they masquerade for truth; and in so doing, I have erected an edifice of self-hate. In what follows, I share some of the illusory truths I have learned about being an Asian American that fuel my self-hate and share how I am taking steps to rewriting those truths so that I may find my way to self-love.

Illusory Truths
Illusory Truth #1: Being Asian is bad

나는 어떤 사람?
나는 좋은 사람?
아님 나쁜 사람?

[What kind of person am I?
Am I a good person?
Or a bad person?]
People — Agust D (*D-2*, 2020)[5]

Ding! Ding! Ding! Three bells mark the end of the elementary school day. A light breeze skips down the hallway, trailing behind me and dozens of my peers as we rush the exit; a veritable stampede of untamed animals. Screams of delight and intense chatter buzz as we all pool around the curb awaiting rides home. I feel a light tap on my shoulder.

"Are you Devin?"

I turn and nod my head absentmindedly, still focused on finding my ride. I hardly see the kid that's talking to me.

"I have a friend that wants to talk to you over there," he says pointing towards the big oak tree.

Before I can respond, I feel a jolting tug at my arm yanking me across the school yard. I only register that the kid is bigger than me, by at least two heads, and evidently stronger than me too. We approach two more big kids. One in a red hoodie repeats the earlier refrain, "Are you Devin?". Again, I nod in the affirmative, this time with a sense of dread. Have I done something wrong? Before I can ask, suddenly, I'm shoved to the ground face first, the weight of my backpack heavy against my neck. Groaning, I turn to my side only to meet the blunt force of the red hoodie kid's foot.

Pain. There is only pain for the rest of my memory. I do not recall when I soiled myself. I do not recall who pulled the boys off me. I do not recall when the campus security came to question me. However, I do recall one last detail.

As the burning in my lungs raged and the fibres of my stomach screamed in agony, I heard: "This chink doesn't deserve to have my name."

This early memory from age six or seven was when I first encountered the notion that I was fundamentally different — that I was Asian. I wondered whether my Asian-ness made me inherently bad. I had no conception at the time of why this might be the case, but older, White kids were accepted; they were popular; they belonged. Thus, I thought they had to be on to something. Over the course of my life, this sentiment that I am Asian, that I am different, and that difference made me lesser than continued to repeat. As these social messages repeated, I could not help but internalise them and come to believe them as true.

Illusory Truth #2: Asians are good at math

> 믿는 게 아냐
> 버텨보는 거야
> 할 수 있는 게 나 이것뿐이라서
> [It's not that I'm believing in it
> I'm just trying to endure it
> Because this is all that I can do]
> *Awake* — BTS (*Wings*, 2016)[6]

With a last name like mine, alphabetically-ordered seating charts always has me near the front of the class. I sit directly to the right of the overhead projector, so I could always smell the faint burning of the lamp; the teacher's fine point, wet erase markers; and the lemon, wholesale brand cleaning solution in the adjacent spray bottle. The day's maths lesson is on fraction addition and subtraction: 4/4ths minus 3/4ths equals 1/4th.

We do a set of practice problems, just like the example, with the teacher as she sits on a cushioned stool in front of the projector; between problems she sprays and wipes off the ink. She invites a couple of students to do practice problems in front of the class. Ashley does 4/5ths minus 2/5ths, Josh does 8/8ths minus 3/8ths, and so on.

"Devin, come up here and try this next problem: 9/12ths + 3/12ths."

I nod and push my chair out to stand. As I make my way to the front someone complains, "It's too easy for him. We all know Asians are good at math."

A few of my peers nod in agreement — derision clear on their faces.

Without batting an eye the teacher replies, "Well, I think Devin can rise to the challenge. Let's see — how about you do this problem then?"

What. Utter. Betrayal.

My heart skips a beat. My palms grow clammy. The hot chills of embarrassment and shame spread up the small of my back to my nape. I already hate doing problems in front of the class. I content myself to solving problems correctly from the comfort of my own desk or at home on homework assignments. I despise having to do something with so many eyes on me. I hate the attention.

The teacher switches out the sheet of transparency film to a blank one, where she could write any problem she wanted. She wrote 4 and 3/12ths - 3 and 2/3rds equals?

I look around. The class immediately goes silent. Of course. Whole numbers!? What are we supposed to do with whole numbers AND fractions? This problem looks impossible to our young elementary minds. All eyes are on me.

Despite some initial apprehension, I stand over the projector, take a deep breath, and scan the problem over again. I think back to what I know about the relation of whole numbers to fractions and think about what the ultimate goal of this problem is asking me to solve. One last *inhale, then on the exhale I touch the tip of the marker down and begin to work. I convert whole numbers into fractions, then convert fractions to like denominators. I write out each step as they come to mind, and in the blink of an eye I produce an answer.*

The teacher smiles and congratulates me on a job well done. The answer is correct. It is such a hollow victory though. None of my peers are impressed. A couple kids in the back roll their eyes, and one says, "Of course he got it right. He's Asian".

I had studied hard to make that moment happen. My race had nothing to do with my solving that problem successfully. And yet, I learned from this moment onward that in certain domains of life, I was only ever going to be a representative of my race. Nothing more. At that moment, my peers were prepared to watch me do one of two things: 1) fail — fail the problem and fail to be a "good Asian" or 2) succeed — solve the problem and reinforce their every notion of what a "good Asian" is. Either way, my failure or success was going to say something about my race; my accomplishments or failures were not my own.

Furthermore, I learned from this moment that my accomplishments were not worth celebrating. Because they came from an apparent, inherent racial advantage, my accomplishments were more of a threat to others than something to be honoured or admired. Something I always imagined would be different had I been born White.

Over time, perceptions of Asian Americans have gone from vilified "yellow peril" to upstanding "model minority".[7] I inhabit the United States at a time in which Asian Americans are viewed as a monolithic people of genius-level mathematical aptitude, filial piety, and uncompromising industriousness. Despite the positive connotations this model minority status presents, I and others like me are still subject to its negative prejudicial, discriminatory, and racial undertones. A genius-level, mathematical Asian American must also be nerdy, unathletic, and uncreative. An Asian American dedicated to family must also be too dependent and unable to think for themselves. An uncompromising, industrious Asian American must also be cruel, cold, and calculated. Asian Americans cannot simply be smart, of strong family values, and hard-working in the United States.[8]

I hated myself for not being able to accomplish something meaningful beyond the expectations of my race.

Illusory Truth #3: Asian food is so weird

> Don't be like a prey
> Smooth like a- like a snake
> 벗어나고 싶은데
> [Though I want to escape]
> *Lie* — BTS (*Wings*, 2016)[9]

Raucous laughter and endless chatter echo throughout the halls of my middle school as I walk towards the cafeteria with my lunch bag in tow. The distinct smells of bleach and square pizza waft past me as I make my way inside. Phil claims a table for us, so I sit across from him as we wait for Brittany, Sarah, and Adam to get through the lunch line. We complain about the challenge of memorising the capitals of Eastern Europe and Central Asia for Social Studies until the rest of our crew has joined us.

As they sit, Phil and I begin to unpack our lunches. He unpacks a lunch of pasta with meat sauce, edamame, and a slice of brownie. I unpack a bowl of white rice, some spicy, sautéed water spinach, and an opaque container that must be the surprise my grandma mentioned as we left for school. I open up the lid and find to my delight a crispy, fried fish head.

While fish heads are particularly bony and a challenge to eat, in my family, they are considered the most coveted part of the fish for its flavour; it is usually saved for our eldest family members to enjoy. For my grandma to go through the trouble of frying fish and saving me a head was so elating and meant a lot to me in a profoundly ineffable manner.

Despite my initial glee, much to my chagrin, the rest of my table responds with faces of utter disgust. "You eat that!?" "Gross, it's looking back at you!" "What's that awful smell!?" "Dude, Asian food is so weird." "Where are you even from that you eat that?"

Embarrassment flushes my cheeks and I quickly close up the fish and put it back in my bag. I swallow the initial joy and vehemently deny my love for the special food. Affixing my own expression with a false hint of disgust, I pack it away and express disbelief that my grandma would make that.

In this moment, I learned that despite being an American my entire life, things core to my being (i.e., the food I eat, the clothes I wear), were always going to be considered foreign, weird, and inferior. The question "Where are you even from?" followed me everywhere I went because of my divergent cultural practices, and I struggled to balance defending these behavioural choices and take pride in who I am with the desire to fit in and not stick out.

I am not alone in inhabiting this strange, marginal space. Many other Asian Americans report experiencing the ills of what is called perpetual foreigner stereotype.[10] Perpetual foreigner stereotype is the assumption that, due to one's minority group membership and different cultural practices, that individual will never be a member of the native group. Being perpetually perceived as a foreigner in your own country has led to experiences of "anxiety, stress, helplessness, academic disengagement, anger, and frustration".[10]

Reflecting on that memory, I'm often struck with a pang of guilt, shame, and regret; not because the food was embarrassing, but because I didn't stand up for my cultural roots; instead I publicly rejected my grandma's love.

I hated myself for not only enjoying cultural practices that stuck out and called unwanted attention, but also for not being able to defend those very practices when they came under scrutiny.

Illusory Truth #4: Asians are not sexy

이 넓은 바다 그 한가운데
한 마리 고래가 나즈막히 외롭게 말을 해
아무리 소리쳐도 닿지 않는 게
사무치게 외로워 조용히 입 다무네
[In the middle of this wide ocean,
A whale talks in a low, calm, and lonely voice
That it can never reach someone else no matter how
hard it shouts,
Feels so lonely that it closes the mouth]
Whalien 52 — BTS (*The Most Beautiful Moment in Life,
Pt. 2, 2015*)[11]

A notification message pops up on my phone screen: "Your profile picture has been approved." I tap the notice and open up the dating app. I'm quite happy with how the photo turns out. A friend of mine insisted on taking a picture of me one day while we were walking his dogs in the park. I'm glad he did. In the photo, I look fun and flirty, and I give an authentic, Duchenne smile that reaches my eyes. It shows off a good part of me.

I start scrolling through some of the dating profiles—

Profile 1: 5'9", 175 lbs, toned, Up for giving you a good time.
"Oh cute," I think to myself. "Oh wait." I read a little further:
"No Asians" it says.
    "Umm... okay." I scroll on.

Profile 2: 6'0", 170 lbs, Love making food, making music, and the outdoors.
"Oh, a cook and musician — how awesome! Oh wait."
"Looking for Whites/Latinos only," the profile goes on to say.
    "Umm... okay." I scroll on.

Profile 3: 6'2", 200 lbs, Bisexual looking for friends and dates.

I read the full description this time before getting my hopes up. I see no indications that I don't somehow fit into what this guy's looking for, so I send him a message. "Hi! The beach in your profile picture looks amazing! How are you doing?" I write.

He answers back almost immediately, "Sorry, not interested in Asians — just my preference." I slam my phone down on my bed. I just want to give up.

I was always told there were "plenty of fish in the sea" when it came to dating, but day after day of similar scrolling past sign posts of such blatant disinterest in my race made it feel like perhaps I was never granted access to "this sea" in the first place. I learned that there was something fundamentally unattractive about my being. How approachable and appealing I thought I was became irrelevant because people wouldn't even give me the time of day.

Part of me wished that this was a unique experience I was suffering alone. Unfortunately, many other gay/bisexual Asian men have reported similar experiences while online dating. An *American Journal of Public Health* report found that Asian and Pacific Islander men who have sex with men experienced more racism within the gay community than their African American/Black or Latino counterparts.[12] In fact, a qualitative study in the *Journal of Sex Research* found that men of colour were aware of an unspoken racial hierarchy, in which White men were the most desirable and "API [Asian and Pacific Islander] men were cast as desexualized and lowest on the sexual hierarchy".[13]

Because of this racialised sexual market, I hated myself for not being attractive.

My path to rewriting illusory truth

These memories distil a complex image of my continuous navigation through social spaces in the United States as a member of a minority racial group. And these are only some representative stories of just one of my minority identities. I am also queer, genderfluid, neurodivergent, and of low socioeconomic status. I could go on at length from my past about my different minority identity experiences and how stereotypes, prejudicial thinking, and social stigma all laid the groundwork for me to loathe myself. But I also want to offer some perspective, some wisdom, and some light that I have earned on my long, still unfolding path to self-love.

Adapt and cope

My first step in the path toward self-love was survival; surviving self-loathing, surviving self-hatred, and surviving the profound perception that I was unwanted, unworthy, and unloved. Survival meant adapting to my present surroundings and conditions as much as possible and learning to cope with the unhappiness. I had learned early on that people did not like me for who I was, so I needed something else to grasp onto. At some point, I had learned that people liked me for the things I could do and this was something worth gripping tightly.

In my youth, I spent an inordinate amount of my personal time volunteering and helping people. I tutored people through years of homework assignments, edited hundreds of papers, offered advice on how to speak with different teachers about different issues, volunteered with retirement homes and seasonal food drives, and listened to hours and hours of people needing to rant, complain, cry, or unload deep secrets. As an adult, I volunteered to work more hours, switch shifts with people, come in early and leave late, and work through lunch. With each action, people praised me for my work and presence, and I thought that meant I had become more wanted, more worthy, more loved.

Idle moments alone made my skin crawl. Left to my own devices, the attentional dam within my mind that held back my worst beliefs and impulses would burst and toxic bile would flood my every thought. *You're not good enough. No one really likes you. You're only good if you keep working, but you're being lazy right now.* To halt the flow of self-torture, I frantically searched for other things to do and prodded others for more opportunities to help. j-hope beautifully captures this sentiment in his upbeat verse in *Dis-ease* (병) (2020) "몸 부서져라 뭘 해야 할 거 같은데" — It feels like I should be doing something to the point my body shatters.[14]

Without realising it, I had internalised toxic capitalist values.[15] I derived my entire sense of self-worth on my productivity and how helpful I could be to others. When I wasn't productive or helpful, I wasn't worthy. I leaned so heavily on what I did instead of who I was. I became a "human doing" rather than a "human being".

Toxic as this can be, this was what I needed at the time to survive. I lived for those fleeting moments of self-satisfaction and self-appreciation for a job well done and a person well helped. Those minor doses of dopamine maintained my workaholism.[16, 17] When I could, I attempted to reduce harm.[18] For me, reducing harm meant setting boundaries for eating, sleep, and leisure time. I was going to continue to feel guilty about not working and continuing to loathe myself for perceived laziness, but establishing those boundaries would save me from my harshest demons.

Eventually, the ecology created by my internalised capitalism became a vicious cycle. I would work to feel good. I would feel good about work and would volunteer to take on more work to feel more good. But I would take on too much and I would fail to balance all of the extra work and fail to perform well. I would feel bad for failing to perform. The feeling of failure would spur me into a depressive episode, and I would feel even worse about not performing my duties. Eventually, I would pull out of the episode and begin again. Slowly doing more and more work until I could not handle it. Something had to give and it needed to start with me.

With the encouragement of friends, I took on one bold act of self-love and re-entered therapy to do the hard work of undoing my unhealthy behaviours and stabilising my life. Engaging in therapy was an explicit acknowledgement to myself that I was worthy of committed time and attention. Through therapy, I built new habits and ways of being that would be instrumental to me finding a way towards self-love.

Write new truths on the wall

After stabilising my life, I had the time and energy to commit to unlearning my illusory truths. Admittedly, I did not know how to start doing this. It was not immediately obvious what was true and untrue about me. Turning to my therapist for advice, she recommended I ask friends and write down what qualities they thought best described me.

I had never truly dedicated time to seeing myself through someone else's eyes. My friends told me that I was "cunning" and "resourceful" and "tasteful" and "smile-inducing" and "beautiful" and so much more. At first, I couldn't believe their words and deflected them, chalking it up to some hyperbolic, inflated sense of me they must have had. Yet they countered each deflection with examples and compelling reasons why these traits were true for me. They insisted I was blocking myself from seeing the real me. Their words cut through my core, leaving me feeling this budding elation that maybe I was indeed wanted, worthy, and loved.

My therapist had made clear that it was not enough to merely have these one-off conversations and write these qualities down and never see them again; I had to incorporate them somehow into my daily life. I decided that I would write down each trait on a neon sticky note and stick that note up on a wall or surface I am sure to see every day. I have two places I dedicate to these messages: the wall beside my bed and the mirror in my bathroom. At first,

I felt ashamed, awkward, and insane for trying to write the things my friends said about me. These words felt untrue and like empty affirmations. But each day I take the time to read them, to become familiar with them, to try them on for size. Some fit great and I feel this newfound effervescence simmer within me. Some don't fit so well and I struggle to integrate that trait or perspective in my mind, but I'm sure I'll come around.

Critical thinking/Contradiction with intention

After plastering my wall with truth statements that my closest friends helped me brainstorm, it came time to reflect on these truths and compare them to what I had previously held true about myself.

My critical thinking process began with writing lists. In one column I wrote all the traits I thought were true of me and in a second column I wrote all the words on my sticky notes. Then I looked across the lists and asked: How could I be "stupid" when my friends, who are reliable sources, say that I am "cunning"/"resourceful"? How could I be "useless" when I am "impactful"? How could I be "weak" when I am "strong"/"resilient"? I didn't have an immediate response, so I let these ideas sit and simmer in a notebook for a few days.

In the meantime, I revisited the chequerboard pattern of neon notes on my mirror and bedroom wall. Every time I brushed my teeth, washed my hands, woke up, or went to bed, I saw these words. They slowly morphed from cold, unknown acquaintances to warm, familiar friends. I didn't necessarily accept them all immediately, but they became increasingly comfortable to identify with. I no longer cringed when thinking about myself as "beautiful".

I returned to my notebook and I pressed myself further: if it's possible I have been wrong about these qualities, am I perhaps wrong about other things about myself? I tried probing: "Why am I unwanted? Why am I unworthy? Why am I unloved?" I supplied these questions with answers: "because I am Asian, because I am queer, because I am unproductive" and so on. I followed this line of thinking with even more questions: "Why is being Asian bad? Why is being queer bad? Why is being unproductive bad?" and so on. Over time, I supplied even more answers: "Because my accomplishments are rubbish, because my food is weird, because I am unattractive" and so on. Eventually, I landed on these questions: "Who told me that this was true? Where did they tell me this? When did this become true?" As I tried to answer, I realised that unreliable sources made me believe this was true, or I inferred this from reactions of people whose credibility was suspect. "Who told me this was true? Where did they tell me this? When did this become true?" And over time, I slowly unearthed the many lessons I had learned from others about the state of my being. I slowly pulled back the curtain on my illusory truths and found them for what they were — falsehoods. My accomplishments couldn't be rubbish — they made me "cunning" and "resourceful". My food isn't weird — through it I became "tasteful". And I'm not unattractive — I'm "beautiful".

In parallel to this process, I worked on my thinking from another angle. I asked myself: "When did I become unwanted? When did I become unworthy? When did I become unloved?" Was it six years old? Seven years old? Eight years old? If I could even give an answer, I followed up with "what did I do at that age that was so undeserving?" I set out to contradict these deeply held beliefs with intention, to compel myself to be specific about reasons and moments that I became unwanted, unworthy, and unloved; only to discover that I had none. One- and two-year-old me were no less deserving than seven- or eight-year-old me and were no less deserving than 27- or 28-year-old me.

Combined, these two exercises in thought helped me bridge the gap between the sticky notes on my wall and my conception of myself. They don't perfectly align nowadays, but they certainly are more consistent. Seeing myself through my closest loved ones' eyes helped me to cast doubt on my worst demons and reshaped the way I looked in the mirror.

Do something

Thinking about and tackling my illusory truths took an immense amount of cognitive effort, emotional energy, and time. I spent several months in relative physical isolation to get where I am now, which is still an active and engaged process of learning to love myself.

In between the moments of self-work and epiphany I started doing things for myself for the mere pleasure of it. I go on long walks to enjoy the fresh air of my neighbourhood, I take occasional drives to my favourite beach and lay out in the sun with a good book, I throw myself random dance parties in my living room, I take bubble baths, I indulge my food cravings, I sometimes brave my kitchen and make myself "weird" food, and I enjoy virtual time with my ARMY family when they're available.

I've come to realise that staying mindful and engaged with my day staves off negative thoughts and dwelling on ill-fortune. Leaving a little time for me to do something I look forward to, no matter how big or small, is part of my ritual of self-care. Self-care is planned for — it's thought of ahead of time. Meanwhile, coping is a response to stress — it's reactionary. I find that the more self-care I work into my day, the less time I spend stressing and coping.

My reflection

Through my self-love journey thus far, I have come to understand three things. First, I have learned that existence is resistance. There will always be people in the world that will find reasons not to like me. They will seek to belittle and disparage me to maintain a sense of superiority; something they think they need to love themselves. But the self-love I am working towards requires no others be put down. The self-love I am cultivating sees myself despite the degradation and recognises the act of resistance it is to embrace being me. Within that I see strength that is worthy of love. Second, I have learned that there will always be people in the world that will find reasons to love me for me. In moments when I felt most alone and in need of reassurance, I took a chance and reached out for help. I was stunned by how many people responded with support and love. It gave me the confidence to lean into my uniqueness, lean into my passions, and lean into love. I found myself leaning so far I practically "trust fell" into the crowd of people who love me for me. I am immensely grateful for these folx. Third, this process has reminded me of one of my favourite sayings: progress is progress. Growth and self-love do not abide by deadlines or steady metrics. They happen when they happen and that incremental movement is worth celebrating. In my academic field, we like to remind each other that development happens in stages, not ages — which is to say that we progress through life on our own time, in our own right. This has been powerful to remember.

When I look in the mirror, I now notice the brands of my self-hatred are barely perceivable; their searing heat has subsided leaving only the faintest of scars. Those words no longer flood my every sense and drive me to look away. The neon sticky notes and the countless lists and pages of writing have made it easier for me to see myself. I don't completely love myself, not yet anyhow, and perhaps not ever. But I have come to embrace and love parts of me that I had not before and that has made all the difference.

Best wishes on your own journeys to self-love. I know I'll keep working on mine. 보라해요! 화이팅!

References

1   BTS. (2016). Reflection [Song]. On *Wings*. Big Hit Entertainment; Doolset. (2018). *Reflection* [Translation]. https://doolsetbangtan.wordpress.com/2018/06/16/reflection/

2   Maragakis, L. (2020, July 15). *Coronavirus, social and physical distancing and self-quarantine.* https://www.hopkinsmedicine. org/health/conditions-and-diseases/coronavirus/ coronavirus-social-distancing-and-self-quarantine

3   Hasher, L., Goldstein, D., & Toppino, T. (1977). Frequency and the conference of referential validity. *Journal of verbal learning and verbal behavior, 16*, 107-112.

4   The Decision Lab. (n.d.). *Illusory truth effect - Biases & heuristics.* https://thedecisionlab.com/biases/illusory-truth-effect/

5   Agust D. (2020). People [Song]. On *D-2*. Big Hit Entertainment; Doolset. (2020). *People* [Translation]. https:// doolsetbangtan.wordpress.com/2020/05/22/people/

6   BTS. (2016). Awake [Song]. On *Wings*. Big Hit Entertainment; Doolset. (2018). *Awake* [Translation]. https://doolsetbangtan. wordpress.com/2018/06/01/awake/

7   Nguyen, J., Carter, J. S., & Carter, S. K. (2019). From yellow peril to model minority: Perceived tThreat by Asian Americans in employment*. *Social science quarterly, 100*(3), 565-577. doi:10.1111/ssqu.12612

8   Ho, C., & Jackson, J. W. (2001). Attitude toward Asian Americans: Theory and measurement. *Journal of applied social psychology, 31*(8), 1553-1581. doi:10.1111/j.1559-1816.2001. tb02742.x

9   BTS. (2016). Lie [Song]. On *Wings*. Big Hit Entertainment;
    Doolset. (2018). *Lie* [Translation]. https://doolsetbangtan.
    wordpress.com/2018/06/16/lie/

10 Huynh, Q., Devos, T., & Smalarz, L. (2011). Perpetual foreigner
    in one's own land: Potential implications for identity and
    psychological adjustment. *Journal of social and clinical
    psychology, 30*(2), 133-162. doi:10.1521/jscp.2011.30.2.133

11 BTS. (2015). Whalien 52 [Song]. On *The most beautiful
    moment in life, pt. 2*. Big Hit Entertainment; Doolset. (2018).
    Whalien 52 [Translation]. https://doolsetbangtan.wordpress.
    com/2018/06/01/whalien-52/

12 Choi, K., Paul, J., Ayala, G., Boylan, R., & Gregorich, S. E.
    (2013). Experiences of discrimination and their impact on
    the mental health among African American, Asian and
    Pacific Islander, and Latino Men who have sex with men.
    American journal of public health, 103(5), 868-874. doi:10.2105/
    ajph.2012.301052

13 Paul, J. P., Ayala, G., & Choi, K. (2010). Internet sex ads for
    MSM and partner selection criteria: The potency of race/
    ethnicity online. *Journal of sex research, 47*(6), 528-538.
    doi:10.1080/00224490903244575

14 BTS. (2020). Dis-ease (병) [Song]. On *Be*. Big Hit
    Entertainment; Doolset. (2020) 병 (Dis-ease) [Translation].
    https://doolsetbangtan.wordpress.com/2020/11/20/dis-ease/

15 Weiss, S. (2016). *5 common behaviors that perpetuate toxic
    capitalism*. https://everydayfeminism.com/2016/11/
    common-behaviors-toxic-capitalism/?mc_cid=7d8121e158

16 Lebowitz, S. (2016, February 02). *A Stanford scientist
    says our culture breeds workaholism -- and it's making*

us sick. https://www.businessinsider.com.au/
stanford-scientist-culture-encourages-workaholism-2016-2

[17] Treadway, M. T., Buckholtz, J. W., Cowan, R. L., Woodward, N. D., Li, R., Ansari, M. S., ... Zald, D. H. (2012). Dopaminergic mechanisms of individual differences in human effort-based decision-making. *Journal of neuroscience, 32*(18), 6170-6176. doi:10.1523/jneurosci.6459-11.2012

[18] Hawk, M., Coulter, R. W., Egan, J. E., Fisk, S., Friedman, M. R., Tula, M., & Kinsky, S. (2017). Harm reduction principles for healthcare settings. *Harmreduction journal, 14*(1). doi:10.1186/s12954-017-0196-4

FROM TEAR TO ANSWER

Brunna Martins

Tear

"The words that I could not bring myself to say flow down"[1]

My journey with self-love started with suffering, and I don't believe it was a coincidence that I met BTS a few weeks before the release of the album Love Yourself: 轉 Tear. In an artistic analysis, in the creation of the Love Yourself era album design, Follador and Maciel interpret the symbol on the cover of the four versions of the second physical disc in the trilogy as follows: "at the bottom, it resembles a leaf, but everything seems confused and shapeless, and it really is that: the feeling of being lost, the petals falling, your world falling apart"[2] During the first months of 2018, it was exactly these sensations that I felt when I started the difficult but necessary journey to recognise my traumas. In this first stage, which I will call 'revelation', I had episodes of sudden and painful clarity related to my last two years in high school and the consequences that had brought me. I was about to turn 18, I had just started my second semester at university, but my body told me there was something wrong. Compulsive crying attacks, derogatory thoughts, tachycardia, shortness of breath, and fainting were symptoms that I'd had since 2016, but that in 2018 were accentuated by the belated awareness that I had been a victim of sexual and psychological violence at the hands of a teacher.

From psychoanalysis, the situation of sexual abuse is understood as traumatic. "Trauma is understood as an excessive situation, experienced by the subject, who, at the moment, is unable to vent this energy load."[3] In the case of trauma experienced by sexually abused children and adolescents, this situation exceeds the child's ability to make sense of what happened. Such findings, in a less scientific and more intuitive way, bombarded my mind for months, and not only internal turbulences, but also external ones, started to modify the illusion of linearity that unfolded my life. Admitting to myself that I had been a victim of something so hideous was like looking in the mirror and seeing the wounds that it had caused me, but the acknowledgement of the people around me demanded other processes, external to me.

According to Arpini, Siqueira, and Savegnago, the victim's inability to reveal what happens, along with the fear of not being understood by close adults, leads to isolation, which further strengthens the experience of helplessness.[3] Because of this, guilt and shame were the feelings that tormented me the most and the trauma was the cause of a distorted perception of myself and the situation. For a teenager who never had much guidance on love and self-love, the naive curiosity about my sexuality had triggered the criminal act and the suffering I was experiencing was the consequence that I would have to bear.

Still during the beginning of 2018, a former classmate, who had been harassed by the same teacher, brought to me the news that he had been denounced and that he was temporarily removed from his duties while the investigation was ongoing. Even unconsciously, I clung to that little thread of hope and, when I realised, I took action. The first time that I told this part of my story to someone was through an audio recording sent by a messaging application. Between crying and sobbing, I summarised two years in ten minutes, not knowing what kind of response to expect. At the time, a former teacher had assumed a position in the administration of the institute where I had studied and she was in charge of the investigation. The feeling was that I was finally purging a toxic virus that was permeating my soul or removing a huge stone from above my body. In any case, I felt hurt, vulnerable and brittle.

Telling my parents didn't come naturally, but it was an inevitable decision given the state I was in. According to Ressel et. al, the phase of adolescence experienced by women is, most of the time, characterised by the repression of their sexuality; by the differentiation of conducts and controls imposed differently to men; by the "no" that indicates the constant limits; by the prohibitions; by the notion of inferiority and passivity, among other conditions; as well as the lack of dialogue and clarification of the biological, social, and cultural events that are part of her life.[4] Facing my family, with whom I first learned that I should reduce myself to fit an accepted standard — reduce my curiosity, my desires, my intuition, and who I am — and revealing that someone had manipulated my naïveté was one of the most painful processes I have ever faced, but it is also one of the most necessary, although I still did not understand it at the time.

Magic shop
"Open the door and this place will await"⁵

According to Rossi, "science, art and religion are among the fundamental constituents of the human person and of culture in general".⁶ The author explains that we all have these three dimensions that are often contradictory and, only with considerable effort, we are able to incorporate them so that there is a minimum of coherence. In the beginning of 2018, when the 'revelation' happened, science was not something that supported me, because it is linked to the rigorous and automatic study routines in my life. I knew I had to graduate from university, have a good job and build a family, but I started to wonder why that was and I couldn't find motivations that would keep me going beyond social pressure. Religion has not been present in my experience for years, since I started to notice that the prejudices rooted in my family members were justified by their church. So I was left with art.

At this point the second stage of my journey with self-love begins and I will call it 'comfort'. When 'revelation' became just a bad event, something that should be forgotten and never remembered, and when science, religion, my family, and friends were not enough for the pain I was carrying to cease, I clung to art. The process of getting to know BTS throughout the turbulent year of 2018, joining the ARMY fandom from platforms like Twitter, and also through new friendships has renewed my social and energetic circle. At first, I was a little scared by the ease with which I found people within ARMY who had been through the same experience as me, or who faced similar situations. In Brazil, sexual abuse is a historical problem, with an alarming number of 17,000 cases in the latest data collected during 2019, however, speaking openly about my experience, without facing the constant fear of being discredited and judged, it was something new.[7]

In September 2018, BTS participated for the first time in a United Nations Assembly, just under a year after launching the global anti-violence campaign Love Myself. From that day and often, I have been listening to the words spoken in RM's speech again, as a kind of 'consultation book', whenever I want to remember or understand again that my voice is necessary in this world: "Now, I insist that they speak for themselves. I would like to ask all of you: What are your names? What excites you and what makes your hearts beat? Tell me your stories, I want to hear your voices and hear your convictions".[8] Researchers Chang and Park say that BTS does not begin with social issues, rather they start with the most personal issues which gradually become more public, first within the group's active communication and then via social media with their fans. This feeds back into their creative work, completing the emotional circle of digital intimacy. This emotion, while not actual action, does provide an inner energy that both impels and lends affective colour to the action.[9] Over time, I began to realise not only how the words of the group comforted me, but also how I struggled to incorporate them. I realised that this was not my own process, but that I shared it with the people around me. Each bond that I formed within the fandom, between daily conversations or links to publications, indirectly said to me: "I'm here to listen to you, because I care and I have affection for you". This happened because we liked the group and were influenced by their conduct, placing trust in each other because we felt safe and belonged to a community.

In *Daring Greatly*, Brené Brown says that the greatest certainty that her training brought her was that "we are here to create bonds with people. We were designed to connect with each other. This contact is what gives our life purpose and meaning, and without it, we suffer."[10] During the beginning of 2019, when everything was apparently working out — I had started working at my first job and was sharing a flat near the university — I went through the worst emotional phase of my life. The solitude of my stay away from home was the trigger for me to go through a strong, depressive crisis and, consequently, to have weakening ties with the people around me. "I am not wanted anywhere" and "why do I stay with those who have no appreciation for my company?" these became recurring thoughts, just as the frequency with which I went to classes and social events decreased dramatically. At that time, my ties to BTS and the ARMY fandom made my survival a little more bearable. According to Chang and Park, from their music and other forms of communication with fans, BTS reveals their personal experiences and reflections, which organically creates an affective consensus of self-improvement that, even in the absence of an activist intention, is still converted into a social intervention through the message of "loving myself/yourself".[9] It was from this consensus that I found the strength to recover.

The announcement of the BTS World Tour Love Yourself: Speak Yourself concerts in Brazil happened in February and I made the decision to take some action to get me out of that state.[11] Of course, at the time, I did not know how to explain the motivation that made me get on a plane for the first time and cross a distance of 2,167 kilometres, to stay at the home of a friend I had met on the internet six months ago. But after a long time, I felt I was doing something good for myself; that I was looking for new and precious experiences; I was, in fact, *living*.

I will always remember the sensation of the cold wind that passed over my face as soon as I left the airport; São Paulo seemed to be welcoming me. I hopped on a bus that took me straight to the neighbourhood where I would stay, I met my friend and it was as if we'd had that bond for a lifetime. Even without knowing the reason, for a few moments that day, I cried without restraint. In the bathroom, on her shoulder or under the pillow, while trying to sleep to go to the show the next day, emotions seemed to overflow from my body. But, finally, it was not sadness. Despite having spent 10 hours standing in a line that never seemed to end, when I looked at the sky on that cold Saturday afternoon, I couldn't feel any other feeling, except happiness. The BTS show is one of my most precious memories and also what I consider to be the realisation of our bond. At a time as disturbing as that, discovering that I could still feel my body radiating good energy was a relief.

Answer: Love myself

"On the path to loving myself, It's what I need the most, I'm walking for myself"[12]

Lima says that the confinement imposed by COVID-19 "has been putting to the test the human capacity to make sense of suffering and challenging individuals and society, in Brazil and across the planet, to promote forms of cohesion that dampen the impact of limit experiences in mental life."[13] The year 2020 was definitely challenging, but I tried to accept it as a difficult break. As with many people, my study and work routines were broken and I could see that, because it was so exhaustive and automatic, it was mentally draining. Based on the illusion of the 'pot of gold at the end of the rainbow', I was walking my path without knowing for sure in which direction to go, but being sure that it was unacceptable to stand still. Only from the confinement required by the pandemic, was I able to experience introspection. From this point on, the third stage of my journey with self-love began and I will call it 'meeting'.

Despite being aware that I was the victim of a heinous crime, guilt always permeated my thoughts, so that I could not see myself as someone I could trust. Arpini states that guilt accompanies the traumatic situation of sexual abuse of children and adolescents, as there are curiosities and infantile desires around the construction of sexuality, making it confusing for the victim to understand how much she is really a victim or, due to her wishes, made the act happen and triggered its repetitions.[3] Sharing this part of my story with the people I developed ties with was fundamental for me to recognise that I was not someone dysfunctional or dangerous, but that, on the contrary, I had cultivated the necessary sensitivity to represent the welcome that I so missed.

During this period of introspection, when I did not have to worry about being beautiful and presentable to go to study and work every day, I also redefined my relationship with my own body. After the 'revelation' of my traumas, I started to use my body as an armour made exclusively so that the people around me could not identify what happened to me internally. My main goal was to mix with the crowd and go unnoticed by the eyes of others. When I no longer needed to use this defence mechanism, I started to see and feel my body with more affection, considering it finally a fundamental part of who I am. The realisation of this made me give my own meaning to the word 'spirituality', which particularly refers to the respect for my physical and psychic limits, to the attention given to the signs that my organism hates, to a food that brings me well-being, the ritual of cleaning and moisturising my skin as a way of taking care of myself, among other habits that I incorporate, day after day, into my routine.

According to Brown, "living fully means embracing life from a feeling of self-love. That means cultivating enough courage, compassion and bonds to wake up in the morning and think, 'No matter what I do today or what I fail to do, I have my worth'".[10] When the 'comfort' provided by art took me to places where I felt safe and welcomed, I was able to walk towards a 'meeting' with myself. Active participation within the ARMY fandom, through initiatives that promote charity, education, and, above all, inspire people to find their own ways, gave me the opportunity to live experiences that made me realise that if we are together for something that gives us purpose, significant changes can be achieved. I identified that I was and still am experiencing something significant, which should be valued: a bond. Little by little, from it, I started to create deep connections with other people; mature, in a way that has been deprived of me for a long time; discover the things that I am able to achieve and, above all, that like any other human being in this world: I also deserve to be loved, even by myself.

References

[1] BTS. (2018). Outro: Tear [Song]. On Love yourself: 轉 Tear. Big Hit Entertainment; Genius. (2018). *Outro: Tear* [Translation]. https://genius.com/Genius-english-translations-bts-outro-tear-english-translation-lyrics

[2] Follador, J. & Maciel, C. (2020, August 12). *LOVE YOURSELF: A arte de criar álbuns*. http://barmysacademicas.com/arte/love-yourself-a-arte-de-criar-albuns/

[3] Arpini, D. M., Siqueira, A. C. & Savegnago, S. (2012). Trauma psíquico e abuso sexual: o olhar de meninas em situação de vulnerabilidade. *Psicologia: teoria e prática*, 14(2), 88-101.

[4] Ressel, L. B., Junges, C. F., Sehnem, G. D. & Sanfelice, C. (2011). A influência da família na vivência da sexualidade de mulheres adolescentes. *Escola anna nery*, 15(2), 245-250.

[5] BTS. (2018). Magic shop [Song]. On Love yourself: 轉 Tear. Big Hit Entertainment; Genius. (2018, May 18). *Magic shop* [Translation]. https://genius.com/Genius-english-translations-bts-magic-shop-english-translation-lyrics

[6] Rossi, C. (2009). Arte e psicanálise na construção do humano. *Ciência e cultura*, 61(2), 25-27.

[7] *Ministério divulga dados de violência sexual contra crianças e adolescentes*. (2020, May 18). https://www.gov.br/mdh/pt-br/assuntos/noticias/2020-2/maio/ministerio-divulga-dados-de-violencia-sexual-contra-criancas-e-adolescentes

[8] BTS. (2018, September 24). *BTS speech at the United Nations | UNICEF* [Video]. YouTube. https://youtu.be/oTe4f-bBEKg

[9] Chang, W., & Park, S. (2019). The fandom of Hallyu, a tribe in the digital network era: The case of ARMY of BTS. *Kritika kultura*.

[10] Brown, B. (2016). *A coragem de ser imperfeito*. Sextante.

[11] Big Hit Labels. (2019, February 19). BTS (방탄소년단) WORLD TOUR 'LOVE YOURSELF: SPEAK YOURSELF' SPOT [Video]. https://youtu.be/r-uN2VzsfXU

[12] BTS. (2018). Answer: Love myself [Song]. On Love yourself: 結 Answer. Big Hit Entertainment; Genius. (2018, August 24). *Answer: Love myself* [Translation]. https://genius.com/Genius-english-translations-bts-answer-love-myself-english-translation-lyrics

[13] Lima, R. C. (2020). Distanciamento e isolamento sociais pela Covid-19 no Brasil: impactos na saúde mental. *Physis: Revista de saúde coletiva*, 30(2), e300214.

DRAWING SPACES

Cindy Nguyen

134340 [planet]: number assigned to mark the demotion of Pluto's existence as a planet to a dwarf planet.

Humans are made of stardust. The atoms that make up our existence came from stars and from supernovas that formed over billions of years and span multiple star lifetimes.[1] The remnants and memories of stars are burned into our being and when you gaze up at a star, you are witnessing stars as they *once* were and much like when you cross paths with another human, they too are a product of the past. We all reflect different histories that bleed into our present. When we breathe in cosmic dust that falls upon Earth every year,[2] the breath that is exhaled then carries a bit of ourselves back to the universe. My first breath, coloured by my Vietnamese heritage, was marked by my parents' fear that I would not be allowed to live freely without restraint in a white dominated society. My Vietnamese name was quickly replaced by an anglicised name so that the legal system can see me as a Canadian. Much like Pluto losing its name and place within the solar system, it feels like my family had to cloak me with a palatable identifier so that I could experience a semblance of belongingness.

Since I was young, rituals of self-care were always embedded within the realm of privilege and as the daughter of a refugee father, the fundamental *idea* of self-care is one that my family could not afford. Fighting for acceptance in a foreign Canada, and white dominated society, my Asian parents instilled in me the belief that *until* we achieve a certain standard of wealth, power, and freedom then we were not allowed to take a pause. For a moment's respite would be detrimental to our survival. And so, I grew up pushing myself to dream bigger and to work harder. While others saw this never-ending drive to do more and *be* more as inspirational and admirable, it took a toll on me slowly. And it was precisely this gradual deprivation that made me miss all the signs. My internal love for myself was dependent on external indicators of success. My self-worth became how worthy I was to society. My eyes were blind to my decline until death greeted a mentor and a friend in the same year, a few months apart. Each loss marred with regret and pain in conjunction with past wounds reopening, I found myself confronted with the harsh concept of self-care and self-love. With my family unequipped to help support me as they themselves have not practised rituals of self-care, I had to seek comfort in my online family — BTS and ARMY.

Pillars of self-care, self-love, and self-help have been built upon the individual's back in a neo-liberal society and context.[3] Blame, failure, and fault then lies with the individual and the society shirks responsibilities of a system that has created foundational conditions that intrinsically prevent deep-rooted self-care. BTS' conceptualisations of self-love and what it means to take care of oneself fundamentally dismantle individualistic roots as they explore collective care,[4] counter-storytelling,[5] and rest as resistance.[6] As I found comfort in BTS and in these revolutionary ideas, I became more reflective and gained courage to actively pursue self-care in spaces that have denied me of something so integral to my health and being. I then began to share my vulnerabilities with my family and friends as a result. This chapter is a declaration — an attestment of my commitment towards accepting my inherent radical existence as a perpetual foreigner and how BTS has acknowledged me in all the ways that I show up in the world.[7]

Mi·kro·kos·mos [noun]: a little world; a submicroscopic world

With the markers of the Canadian identity being so intimately tied to whiteness, the kaleidoscope of colours that the galaxy painted my atoms with must be filtered and muted so that when the white centre of society gaze upon me, they are not reminded of how the historical oppressions that they enacted are still carried out today, much like how there is an insistence to forget that the stars we see are most probably dead.

The state of perpetuity is one framed by concepts of *eternity* and *forever*. When this state is linked to feelings of being a foreigner, no matter how much stardust is shared, equity-seeking communities might as well be galaxies away. The perpetual foreigner syndrome posits that visible minorities will invariably be perceived as a foreigner in a society that is white dominated and this persistent feeling has defined who I am, what my values are, and how my self-care is shaped.[7] My personal well-being is intrinsically tied to the manifestation and preservation of social injustices. I do not carry the privilege of living a life that is not tinged with scars of insidious power structures oppressing me. Social injustices are acts of violence that linger as trauma, and saddle one's being with the weight of enduring mental health impacts and negatively "... impact communities and the individual identities within them".[8] The heavy burden that I bear as a BIPOC individual navigating the white reality, while my coloured reality is denied, is why I pursue placemaking. There is a nagging need for me to prove myself, and to prove my worth. The intensity to draw spaces where I can breathe in all the colours of a nebula. The intensity to revolutionise and shift the tides of dominance. The intensity to *declare* that the stardust in my body *does* belong here and that I *can* and *should* change the world to make a place for myself. The call to be recognised manifested in me being deeply entrenched in social justice work and was why I initially became attached to BTS' music.

BTS stands for Bangtan Sonyeondan and their name symbolises a foundation of artistic integrity towards "...blocking out stereotypes, criticisms, and expectations that aim on adolescents like bullets, to preserve the values and ideal of today's adolescents" and that has continually resonated throughout their career.[9] Their discography laments the state of society while centring and weaving their authentic stories into songs that call people into a space where we recognise each other. When BTS member V wrote *Blue & Grey* based on his feelings of burnout, he expressed that his intention in sharing how he felt during his lowest point was to ask:

You're depressed lately? Me too. We're in the same boat. Wanna talk about how you're feeling? You wanna feel better, right? I know, but sometimes it feels like you're being washed away by a whirlpool of stress.[10]

As a listener, I found solace. It felt like someone was sitting with me in my sadness so that we could keep each other company. It was a space where we both accepted emotions that were hard to embrace.

BTS' openness and vulnerability display a raw strength that is built with others and is found together. This is collective care. This is what we *need* to counteract neo-liberalistic tendencies to frame self-care as an individual's sole duty. Collective care is built upon the principles of mutual aid where we promise to look after one another and explains that a "...member's well-being — particularly their emotional health — [is] a shared responsibility of the group rather than the lone task of an individual."[4] I learnt that collective care was paramount for those involved in social justice work. I learnt and saw this concept come to life as my mentors, friends, and loved ones embraced me in this space. I learnt that when I find myself weary and tired of insidious systems that refuse to change, I find comfort in RM's "I believe in your galaxy, ARMY", because I know that his reference to *your* actually means *our*.[11] That my galaxy includes a space co-created by BTS, ARMY, and my loved ones. I learnt that it is possible to create a mikrokosmos where I have a place in a little world that centres collective care. This little world where I do not need to prove my existence and worth. The stardust here shines the brightest and I can now recognise everything that has brought me to burn out as a social justice advocate and how to remedy that so that I can find resiliency in being alighted.

Sin·gu·lar·i·ty [noun]: the state, fact, quality, or condition of being singular

As part of the *Grammy Museum's at Home Series*, BTS got interviewed by Scott Goldman where he pointed out that the group have always "...addressed issues that are personal, hardships, societal pressures, mental health" and pointed out that "...this is not the norm for K-pop artists" but that others are starting to follow suit.[12] He then specifically asks Suga, "Why is it important to you and the group to continue to be so vulnerable in the music that you make?" which prompts Suga in replying:

We didn't really think of it that way, that showing our vulnerabilities were important. But we did start from the question, 'why aren't people talking about these issues?'. Maybe it was the positive songs I heard as a kid. I didn't want the music I listen to or the music I make to be violent or not have any message. I thought to myself, if the person who writes a song doesn't talk about their story, then what else would that person write about? Then who would? I felt it was unfortunate that these stories were not being told.[12]

What BTS is showcasing is one's dedication to the art of storytelling and the practise of *authentically* telling stories that are dismissed, misunderstood, or hidden. They are engaging in recognitive justice which is the politics of recognition. They challenge the status quo and question what society deems as normative. This is courage work. The type of work that took me a lot of time to fully enter and is still something I am continuously growing into.

I pursued an education in social work because of my dedication to transformative change and placemaking. I sought out a master's degree because I knew that the higher the education, the more armour I would have to protect myself in this work. My knowledge and words would be validated by an academic institution steeped in whiteness and thus my education became a tool for me to defend myself with when others questioned my credibility. However, I could not help but carry feelings of guilt that I had somehow abandoned myself by reinforcing white knowledge as the only knowledge. How was defining my self-worth on external accolades detrimental to my internal perception of self? How do I reconcile my need to be a revolutionary while recognising that I need to somewhat play the game to enact change? Eaglehawk describes the revolutionary journey as an "...upwards moving spiral which starts at 'love yourself' and has no particular end in sight", but it is precisely this continuously moving spiral that trips me up as I reach up to the stars and expand my mikrokosmos.[13] It is not an easy path. Eaglehawk mentions a loop in the spiral where one's place in the world is celebrated and for myself, the answer was to engage in 'counter-storytelling' as a form of self-care and healing and to acknowledge that it is a process intimately tied to an internal validation of words and honouring of experiences.[13] Much like BTS weaving their feelings, thoughts, and stories into their lyrics, notes, and songs, I wanted to find that freedom for myself as well and to have this step be my grounding anchor. One that can keep me from slipping down this revolutionary spiral. Counter-storytelling would also allow me to be recognised on a social justice level because my personal *is* political. This chapter is an example of the *way* I want to share my story. Sharing a piece of my inner world, means that I will not be able to take it back. It is knowing that the framing of immigrant struggles is often crafted to sell to the white audience and instead of giving specific examples of *why* I feel like a perpetual foreigner, it should be accepted as truth. The concept and the resulting impacts of this syndrome have been explained to build awareness. That should be enough.

There is too much dependence on equity seeking communities to share their story to *teach* and I should not have to use my story to let a white person *see what it's like* to be in my shoes. Because the reality is, a white person will never be able to relate to BIPOC experiences, and they should not try to in order to do something about the injustices we face. I should not bear the burden of teaching to ask for empathy. My counter-storytelling roots itself in recognitive justice much like BTS where we are fighting for recognition within wider systems. A recognition of hope, healing, and desire where "desire is about longing, about a present that is enriched by both the past and future..it is not only the painful elements of social and psychic realities, but also the textured acumen and hope".[14] BTS' music encapsulates messages of freedom, powerful visions of betterment, and inspires dreams. They acknowledge hurt and pains but they also encourage listeners to take a pause to rest and reflect, in order to walk, run, and sprint towards a new self-defined future. Lyrics from *Spring Day* "The morning will come again, no darkness, no season can last forever",[15] *Love Yourself* "The me of yesterday, the me of today, the me of tomorrow (I'm learning how to love myself), with no exceptions, it's all me",[16] and *A Supplementary Story: You Never Walk Alone* "These wings sprouted from my pain, but these wings are going towards the light, even if it's tiring and painful, I will fly if I can, will you hold my hand, so that I won't be afraid anymore?"[17] all lace steady determination, to be wholly authentic in reconciling pain, with desire.

My personal experiences are tied to systems and I should not have to divulge details and water down my complex realities in order to be heard. My power lies in *how* I choose to tell my story. I am more than a pain narrative. I am imbuing my personhood into the words that run across these pages and as your eyes sweep over them, I am leaving a call to action where you are encouraged to reflect on your own positionality and personhood. Do you recognise the dual realities that I live within as a BIPOC individual situated in a white centred world? Do you recognise the relief and rejuvenation I found in collective care? Do you recognise what needs to be changed in order for equity-seeking communities to expand their own safe mikrokosmos? Turn these reflections into *action*.

Le concisely outlines two values that need to be given *back* to storytellers:

Trust asks us to believe the people who are most affected by an unjust system, to take their words at value, even if it's outside our understanding of ability to relate...*Justice* demands that we support those who are most affected by injustice, whether or not we understand or feel empathy for them. It demands the recognition that our thoughts and feelings are secondary, if not irrelevant, to the realities facing many people with whom we will never completely empathise.[18]

While there is a singular aspect of storytelling, it is an active form of knowledge sharing and it connects others to similar yet different experiences. It is cathartic but it can also feel like one is exposing too much because there is a lack of anonymity to protect one's stories. It takes a lot of internal work to make the private visible and there is a lack of knowing how the listener or audience will respond.[19] There needs to be a balance between *sharing* an experience versus trying to *prove* an experience and for the longest time, all I was trying to do was prove myself. Relieving this tension within counter-storytelling empowered me to recognise myself while unquestionably staying true to my singular existence within this expansive world.

Par·a·dise [noun]: an intermediate state or place of bliss, felicity, or delight

When I lost my mentor and a friend within a few months of each other, I used productivity as a distraction. I pushed myself to keep juggling a practicum, classes, and two part-time jobs. I had expectations to exceed, I had goals to achieve and I had items to check off my list. What helped me first, was my growing understanding of collective care and how I started to learn that when burdens are shared, they are not as heavy as they would be when carried alone. I was then able to express my pains *and* desires more openly which translated to storytelling. But the last step that seemed to be the hardest to take was resting. Creating a little world of my own with others was something actionable. The practise of storytelling was something I could develop. Rest was an elusive concept that I had to continually reflect on until it made sense. RM stated in one of his live broadcasts that he came to understand that "The world must become a place where the act of loving myself shouldn't require permission from another. If I can't change the world, then I must change myself".[20] Revisiting this quote, I began to realise that while I was making progress in taking care of myself, I needed to become a *practising* revolutionary. Eaglehawk states that "being a revolutionary is a daily practice, something which can never be mastered, as the nature of the revolution is fluid and nuanced" and a "...21st-century revolutionary is one who firstly changes themselves, before seeking change elsewhere".[21]

Taking a break is not giving up. Changing myself to practise inclusive and radical self-care alongside changing systems is not me giving in. Changing the internal message of "I *should* change the world to make a place for myself" into "I *want* to change the world to make a place for myself and others" frames this as a desire rather than an obligation. This becomes a wish that simmers as fuel rather than an all consuming flame that exhausts. This stems from an understanding that the system is intentionally designed to shut down voices and to tire out equity-seeking communities. Until these external conditions change, it is fair to protect oneself by resting as a form of resistance, especially when the human worth is equated to productivity in a neo-liberal context.[6] Hersey asserts that "resting is a meticulous love practice" and it is a "...spiritual practice, a racial justice issue and a social justice issue".[6] Resting is an act of defiance. An act that disrupts Western societal expectations of continuous progression that hinges on fallible narratives of individuals being limitless and resources that are everlasting. We see this assertion to *do more* and *be more* as determination, but it ultimately becomes extractive when we do not understand the concept of conditions. We excavate and open ourselves up to productivity because that's all we know. BTS' *Dis-ease* grapples with the value of work ethics and one's inability to rest:

> Even our hearts need a vacation
> Oh, just do your job like it's one
> I'm ill, yeah, I'm the job itself
> The friend called 'rest', oh, I never liked him
> How much do you have to earn to be happy?
> This glass bottle hits your head
> Is the world sick or am I sick? I'm confused[22]

Member j-hope speaks to his love-hate relationship with work through *Dis-ease* and laments that while he was working, he would wish for a break but when the group took time off, he felt an urge to work.[23] The guilt associated with this push and pull wracks one's mind and body much like a disease. This inner turmoil illustrated my struggles poignantly and I felt a sense of relief to know that BTS felt similarly. This collective experience of wanting to rest but not knowing how to, is a symptom of productivity culture. The effervescent light that permeates the stardust that resides in us must be protected; for the beauty in our existence is valuable. The fact that we are alive and that we make up the constellations of the world should be enough. We need to be practising revolutionaries that ignite together, because your radiance is reflected in me, and mine in yours.

I have begun to incorporate forms of rest to heal within my mikrokosmos shared with others. I look for the mundane and trivial things that bring contentment. I am reminded with BTS' *Paradise* that it is okay to quietly exist:

> There's no need to run without even knowing the reason
> It's alright to not have a dream
> If you have moments where you feel happiness for a while
> It's alright to stop
> Now we don't run without knowing the destination
> It's alright to not have a dream
> All the breaths you breathe are already in paradise[24]

I open my eyes and look around. I shake my head to clear my tunnel vision. I honour my coloured breaths and smile as I accept all that I am and those who have a piece of my being. When my mother brings me cut fruit to show that she cares, I take a moment to remember these acts of kindness. I take a moment to reflect on how I always compared my parents' expressions of love to white norms while growing up. Always wondering why I do not receive words of love and physical affection which turned into resentment. I regret those moments. Because while my mother was painting stars in my galaxy with her colours, I was covering them with a white veil. It is a shame I admit, for her colours are iridescent, stunningly complex and I doubt I will be able to truly see the everchanging shimmers. But I can try and I can welcome my parents into my rituals of self-care. We will create this paradise together. We will rest and endure. And we will be everlasting.

When I feel disheartened from the injustices of the world, I remind myself that this is a life-long journey and that I need to heal to be able to fight again tomorrow. But until the fight starts again, just existing is enough. Being here is enough. I do not have to be remarkable to matter. I need to create my own sense of paradise in order to heal and rest *is* resistance.

E•ter•nal [adjective]: lasting or existing forever; without end or beginning

My rituals of self-care have been shaped by my pains but ultimately designed for my hopes and desires. It is knowing that a nebula is fascinating and ethereal because it is a *collection* of precious dust and gas and that it provides a home for stars to gleam and glow *together*.[25] It is knowing that there is magic when lives are intertwined and linked through authenticity. It is knowing that by virtue of being alive, the stardust in us makes us a treasure to behold and that we all have a one-of-a-kind, without equal existence that cannot be defined by hollow identifiers such as *134340*. It is in telling our stories the way we want them that we disrupt insidious brandings of who we *should* be in the eyes of Western society. It is understanding that we are more than the pain of our past and present and that our future can be painted with the everflowing charm of the cycle of a new moon. It is in embracing our voice and who we are that we heal in storytelling. It is sharing our *singularity* that leaves a mark in our own distinct *mikrokosmos*. It is in reconciling with rest that we greet each day renewed and it is in bringing others into this *paradise* that we endure and thrive together. It is in gratitude that BTS have become my guide as we both walk side by side up the spiral of self-care and revolutionary practice. Together they are not seven — RM, Jin, Suga, j-hope, Jimin, V, and Jung Kook — and I am not alone. Together we are bulletproof and *eternal* in drawing spaces.

References

[1] Lotzof, K. (n.d.). *Are we really made of stardust?* Natural history museum. https://www.nhm.ac.uk/discover/are-we-really-made-of-stardust.html

[2] Worrall, S. (2015, January 28). *How 40,000 tons of cosmic dust falling to Earth affects you and me.* National geographic.

[3] Michaeli, I. (2017). Self-Care: An act of political warfare or a neoliberal trap? *Development (Society for international development), 60*(1-2), 50-56.

[4] Mehreen, R., & Gray-Donald, D. (2018, August 29). *Be careful with each other.* https://briarpatchmagazine.com/articles/view/be-careful-with-each-other

[5] Solórzano, D. & Yosso, T. (2002). Critical race methodology: Counter-storytelling as an analytical framework for education research. *Qualitative Inquiry, 8*(1), 23-44.

[6] Hersey, T. (2021, January 11). *Our work has a framework.* https://thenapministry.wordpress.com/

[7] Huynh, Q., Devos, T., & Smalarz, L. (2011). Perpetual foreigner in one's own land: Potential implications for identity and psychological adjustment. *Journal of social and clinical psychology, 30*, 133–162.

[8] Lavoie, S. (2021, January 18). *How social justice and mental health interconnect.* University of Calgary.

[9] Trabasso, G. (2016, May 29). *BTS is tackling problems that are taboo.* Affinity magazine. http://affinitymagazine.us/2016/05/29/its-about-time-you-know-why-bts-is-trending/

[10] Kang, M. (2020, November 25). *V "I wish we were back with ARMY, laughing together".* https://magazine.weverse.io/article/view?lang=en&colca=1&num=58

11 Kim, N. [@BTS_twt]. (2016, August 30). *I believe in your galaxy, ARMY!* [Tweet]. Twitter. https://twitter.com/bts_twt/status/770 678677847756800?lang=en

12 SweetNightLover. (2020, September 24). *BTS – Grammy museum interview 200924.* [Video]. YouTube. https://www. youtube.com/watch?v=scGpFxuvJu4&t=130s

13 Eaglehawk, W. (2020). I am ARMY, I am revolutionary. In Eaglehawk, W & Lazore, C (Eds.), *I Am ARMY: It's time to begin* (pp. 113-136). Bulletproof.

14 Tuck, E., & Yang, K. W. (2014). R-words: Refusing research. *Humanizing research: Decolonizing qualitative inquiry with youth and communities*, 223-248.

15 BTS. (2017). 봄날 (Spring day) [Song]. On *You never walk alone.* Big Hit Entertainment; Genius. 봄날 (Spring day) (English translation) [Translation]. https://genius.com/Genius-english-translations-bts-spring-day-english-translation-lyrics

16 BTS. (2018). Answer: Love myself. On Love yourself 結 answer. Big Hit Entertainment; Genius. *Answer: Love myself (English translation)* [Translation]. https://genius.com/Genius-english-translations-bts-answer-love-myself-english-translation-lyrics

17 BTS. (2017). A supplementary story: You never walk alone. On *You never walk alone.* Big Hit Entertainment; Genius. *A supplementary story: You never walk alone (English translation)* [Translation]. https://genius.com/Genius-english-translations-bts-a-supplementary-story-you-never-walk-alone-english-translation-lyrics

18 Le, V. (2020, July 13). *Why we need to move away from empathy in our fundraising approach.* https://nonprofitaf.com/2020/07/why-we-need-to-move-away-from-empathy-in-our-fundraising-

approach/?fbclid=IwAR3nxAoAkPcb4YnnBzUL8CgIUHtZN
M9O10pOnR3OFMHubCwg82Byvk69UU0

19 Lapadat, J. C. (2017). Ethics in autoethnography and collaborative autoethnography. *Qualitative inquiry, 23*(8), 589–603. https://doi.org/10.1177/1077800417704462

20 [@chookook]. (2020, April 12). [Tweet]. Twitter. https://twitter.com/chookook/status/1249408608238030851

21 Eaglehawk, W. (2020, July 16). *We, like BTS, are revolutionaries.* https://medium.com/revolutionaries/we-like-bts-are-revolutionaries-15caae19b7a3

22 BTS. (2020). 병 (Dis-ease). On *Be.* Big Hit Entertainment; Genius. 병 (Dis-ease) (English translation) [Translation]. https://genius.com/Genius-english-translations-bts-dis-ease-english-translation-lyrics

23 Kang, M. (2020, November 24). *j-hope "Even just one, single love is beautiful, but we're getting love from all over the world".* https://magazine.weverse.io/article/view?num=57&lang=en

24 BTS. (2018). 낙원 (Paradise). On Love yourself 轉 tear. Big Hit Entertainment; Genius. 낙원 (Paradise) (English translation) [Translation]. https://genius.com/Genius-english-translations-bts-paradise-english-translation-lyrics

25 Space Center Houston. (2020, March 19). *What is a nebula?* https://spacecenter.org/what-is-a-nebula/

FACING MYSELF

Jacinta Bos

"I'm looking at you in the mirror, the fear-ridden eyes, asking the question"[1]

For a very long time, I did not let myself touch my face. This may seem unusual, but for people experiencing acne, it's common sense. I associated my acne with my hands and the assumption of being a stereotypical, unclean adolescent. This was further compounded by coronavirus telling me that my hands were germ factories, and I could not touch my face once more. It took me a year, one whole year, to discover that stress inflicted my acne. Ironically, the same stress was perhaps brought about by the acne, or even coronavirus itself. The very act of not touching my face, arguably, went on to create a vicious cycle of acne and self-loathing. This is a chapter about my recent epiphany, with its links to my appearance and exposure to life as a young person. Only when I turned inward and introspected, did I find the answers I was looking for, and a way to heal both my acne and my inner self.

As I write this chapter over late 2020 and early 2021, I am in the midst of college life at the age of 17. Throughout my time at college, I expect to face many challenges, more than simply furthering my education. I have always been soft spoken and I valued independence over socialising. After my four years at high school where I gradually grew relationships with people, college made me restart. An unsettling feeling returned, which was heightened by the mix of social hierarchy and beauty norms. As Eaglehawk states, "our childhood, while we negotiate the often turbulent social landscape of primary school and beyond, is where the persona is initially formed".[2] I was lost within the school campus, filled with glaring students, and I soon became alienated from my persona.

Social media has a heavy impact on young people, Henriques and Patnaik write that the "obsession with physical features reveals a lack of holistic perception of self generated subconsciously, following an "outside" standard of beauty not defined by the "inner self" of the receiver".[3] My persona became a mask for my insecurities, as I attempted to chase acceptance at school. My style of clothing became whatever covered my insecurities. In order to fit into a society fuelled by social media, my insecurities must not be visible online; this further compounds the persona alienation. I'm not showing who I really am, so who am I really? This fed into and overlapped with the persona I developed at school. Looking back, I can see how fake the persona I hid behind was. All so I could cover my acne and my low self-esteem.

Prior to the call for this autoethnographical essay, I had sat at what seemed like a form of rock bottom.[4] 2020 brought about coronavirus and a general mood of depression, which has continued into 2021. I was faced with severe social anxiety when I transitioned to a new school environment. Upon entering the year of 2020, I longed to be someone who no longer suffered from acne.

Hazarika's 2016 study of adolescents with acne claims that "the degree of difficulty in daily activities showed statistically significant association to the grade of acne".[5] This helped me understand why the appearance of my face had become the sole decider in my everyday life. My insecurities were heightened and negative thoughts regarding my appearance and, therefore, self-worth, controlled my life. Looking after my skin by means of a skincare routine became an act of punishment instead of a self-care ritual. This led to a chain reaction of deprivation that further damaged my self-esteem. Every morning became repetitive as I would wake up hoping my skin had cleared enough for my makeup to cover it. According to Hazarika, those experiencing acne will do just about everything in their power to camouflage it, such as avoiding eye contact and growing their hair longer to cover their faces.[5] To my surprise, every morning my skin was not up to my impossible expectation. So I battled with my self-worth. I had no confidence to face anybody, including myself.

School was a constant suffering. On my best days, I had just enough strength to study and focus in class. Otherwise, I tried extensively to make myself seem non-existent, avoiding classes for independent study. I look back now and can see how disconnected I became from the world around me and ultimately within myself. I sought help, and counselling became a safe haven amongst the intimidating hallways of school where I could talk freely about my worries without judgement. Yet my mind was not convinced to explore self-love or care any further. To witness my own family book restaurant tables without me, knowing my anxiety would heighten at such an outing, tore at my heart. When times got really bad, skipping school felt like my only option. I became comfortable with coronavirus' restrictions that kept students studying remotely.[6]

But when students returned to campus, I continued to study from home. From confining myself in my room all day to all night and through the next day, I became more and more depressed.

Cross writes "sometimes, we need a short admission to 'calm our mind', in the true sense of the word 'asylum'".[7] I was confined to my home, to calm my mind, which inevitably became my asylum. In my attempt to hide my face from the world, I concealed more from myself. I buried my chance of self-love deeply beneath the chance to fit into society's standards. I feel that teens, like myself, are shown a distorted view of beauty through social media, which is experienced perhaps differently in comparison to other age groups. We "spend an average of nine hours a day using media", and therefore have a heightened exposure to marketing and messages often targeted directly at us.[8] Beauty standards are normalised far and wide through "the media [which] is a dominant means for transmitting and reinforcing cultural beliefs and values [...] [though] it might not be exclusively responsible for determining the standards for physical attractiveness."[9] We are a major market and "are exposed to over 25,000 ads in a year [...] [by] companies [who] spend over $17 billion a year on marketing toward children and teens."[9] Even while I isolated at home and even while my peers led different lives returning to school, we were all being sold the same beauty standard; one which didn't include a face baring imperfection.

Suffering from intense social anxiety caused me to lose my grasp on friendships I had no strength to hold onto. Maybe the weakness I felt was drawn from constant diet changes to morph my body figure into a more acceptable shape. I knew my thoughts that encouraged my destructive ways towards my body were surely influenced by media standards and norms. My want for alone time soon grew into a need to regain strength as I had no energy to socialise from the exhaustion of anxiety attacks. As my gaze focused upon the mirror in the morning and shifted to fix at my feet throughout the day, I began to look at myself from others' point of view over my own.

Eaglehawk writes that "we use our imagination to see how others view us and adjust accordingly in order to fit in."[2] I became stuck in a cycle of viewing myself through other people's eyes to the point that it tortured and tormented me. I was disoriented, and I drifted further and further away from the life I dreamt to live. I previously had shown my smile as an emblem of my true character, yet in 2020 I utilised it as a mask to hide away my social anxiety.

I had discovered BTS at the conclusion of their *Love Yourself* trilogy in the beginning of 2019 and gained an interest in their story. The group's genre of K-pop is not widely known or appreciated in my local area. I hid this aspect of myself, liking BTS, away from the fear of judgement. I let society's normalisation of English music genres shape how I shared and expressed my own music taste. When I listened to BTS, I felt on top of the world, and most importantly, I caught a glimpse of self-love through their eyes. According to Wickman, "the underlying theme of the *Love Yourself* series [is that] before you can truly love someone else, you must first be able to love yourself."[10] This message was soon to profoundly impact my life and give me the chance to learn how to love myself through loving BTS. To love myself, I needed to face my lowest state in order to grow self-awareness. 2020 was a life hurdle, BTS accompanies me as I, now, come over and into the light of self-love.

Subsequently, my discovery of BTS soon brought an introduction to Wallea Eaglehawk and her work. Her book, *Idol*

Limerence drew my attention, and my comprehension of who I am grew exponentially when I read it. Her words opened my eyes to a new perspective of myself and took me through an introspection of the type of love I was experiencing. As someone who initially held a strong affection for my idols, BTS' music began to transform my idol limerence into self-love. Eaglehawk writes that limerence is a "feeling that comes before romantic love [...], it is said to be the strongest of all emotions."[2] Adding to this, in the context of BTS, idol limerence is a form of limerence experienced towards an idol and "only exists when unrequited, therefore, can be without end."[2] Fans of BTS, ARMY, such as me, "sought to love themselves better, at the request of their idols."[2] The euphoric relationship between BTS and ARMY allowed the *Love Yourself* trilogy to inspire self-love as a global movement. As someone who is not surrounded by fellow fans, the lyrics of every song felt like a message sent directly to me. I learnt from Eaglehawk that "this kind of love should surely be able to thwart every other viable relationship of BTS; idol limerence makes one feel as if anything is possible, mostly because it is."[2] With the call for chapters for this book, I knew this is what I needed to push myself forward in the journey of self-love. I am a self-professed people pleaser who hates the thought of oversharing, so to publish a chapter solely written on the topic of loving myself is a step that takes a lot of confidence to accomplish.

Regarding BTS' key message of love yourself, Wickman says that "everyone wants to paper over their faults and focus on those 'loveable' aspects of themselves. Until you accept those darker aspects of yourself, the shadows among the light, the 'self' you love won't be your true self but an idealised version."[10] Through BTS, I learnt that I only need that acceptance from myself. I knew I could only draw a self-love for myself, from myself.

"I'm not afraid because it's me"[1]

The "physical love language", was something I steered away from, as I feared touching my face, but it turns out to be a language which now seems necessary.[11] Feeling insecure about my unsightly hands, it felt necessary to conceal them the same way I learnt to with the rest of my insecurities. But then Jung Kook's song, *Euphoria*, brought my attention, through its lyrics, "take my hands now", to how my hands and touch can help in my self-care.[12] Emblematic of offering support, BTS' words became a guide on my journey of self-love. My hands became an instrument for the expression of care.

I learnt the impact of holding my head within my own hands without the fear of inflammation of acne. Self-comfort created an epiphany for my body ownership. Through the physical love language, your hands are the messengers of your heart. The extensive use of hand sanitiser, due to coronavirus, caused eczema on my hands. Of course, my anxiety played its part causing excessive scratching which made the eczema more obvious. My idealism of "glass skin" or even some form of skin clarity, encouraged me to hide more of myself.[13] As hands are a symbol for a tool of life, I was insecure of the very feature that crafted my own. Nature's mark of identification became something I wished to conceal, again hiding my individuality.

As I am yet to experience a romantic type of love, I focused on the language of self-love.[14] Adolescence caused a wave of insecurities upon my physical appearance, and so to love myself, I learnt that I should be gentle with my body. In relieving my insecurities, I let go of heavy stress, consequently healing my skin. Through valuing self-care, I learnt to love both my inner and outer self. As a people pleaser who fears the disappointment of others, I have begun to learn my worth as an individual and not allow others' mistreatment of me to sway how I feel about myself.

I'm ironically a photographer who is afraid of self-portraiture. Overthinking and constantly criticising myself in a picture steered me away from being in front of the camera. This self-criticising mindset had to change to allow self-love. Because I hated my past self and constantly chased improvement, I never documented my changes. I became oblivious to how much I had grown in the space of 2020 alone. I discovered the antidote for my low self-esteem by creating art which became a passion that drove me to confidence. My very own happiness drew a new standard for me to live up to. From my eyes, I hold beauty, within my independence. So, I now understand that I do not need others' point of view to determine my true beauty because confidence is what makes my heart race. Learning to embrace myself through the practice of self-portraiture is helping me to not be afraid of myself.

"I'll answer with my breath, my path"[1]

Throughout 2020 as BTS became bigger and I began to hear about them more in my local area, I became more hopeful. It was then that I realised how BTS' growing acceptance by the global community made me believe that acceptance for who I am is possible. When the world accepts BTS, they are affirming who I am as ARMY, who I am as me. From here, I began to realise that happiness, like the kind I feel when I listen to BTS or take photos, is integral to self-love.

BTS' *Answer: Love Myself*, from their album, *Love Yourself: Answer*, became an anthem as I sang the English line "you've shown me I have reasons; I should love myself".[1] It was as if I was thanking them for the push they had given me to travel further, not physically but in my journey of self-love. Breaking apart the English translations of the lyrics, I was struck with the realisation of how it relates to me and my journey. "I'm looking at you in the mirror, the fear-ridden eyes, asking the question" relates directly to how my gaze focused daily onto a mirror, as I looked upon myself, afraid to ask how I really felt.[1] Scared to let my exact emotions be expressed.

As the journey of self-love is based on reflection, I learn that I should not look upon who I wish to be but how far I have come and how I should view myself presently. "Loving myself might be harder than loving someone else".[1] It has taken me 17 years to get to where I am today, pushing through the hardship that adolescence brings, and the expectations society puts on me. I believe that I am not near my end of this venture as my mind has only just begun to accept the thought of self-love. So my first step was to love my own skin in all its beauty as the line reads "why do you keep trying to hide under your mask? Even all the scars from your mistakes make up your constellation".[1]

Jacinta is not a common name. Yet hearing it more often as I grew older, my name began to lose value. I now see my name as a gift of identity that was given to me at birth by my parents. As RM said at the 2018 UN speech, "find your name, find your voice by speaking yourself".[15] I wish to create my own self in which I am titled by my own name and character.

Knowing that others will come to read this chapter, makes me wonder how different perspectives will compare their experiences to mine. The thought that there could be a possible benefit towards a person reading this, gives me confidence in my own growth. I do not know what the future holds, for everything is just as uncertain as ever. But as BTS have taught me, life does indeed go on, whether we like it or not. All we truly have is the present, so I shall love myself in all the glory of now.

References

1   BTS. (2018). Answer: Love Myself [Song]. On *Love yourself Answer*. Big Hit Entertainment; Doolset. (2018). *Answer: Love myself* [Translation]. https://doolsetbangtan.wordpress.com/2018/08/24/answer-love-myself/

2   Eaglehawk, W. (2020). *Idol Limerence: The art of loving BTS as phenomena*. Revolutionaries.

3   Henriques, M., & Patnaik, D. (2020). *Social media and its effects on beauty*. https://www.intechopen.com/online-first/social-media-and-its-effects-on-beauty.

4   Eaglehawk, W. (2020). *Love yourself [Closed] — Revolutionaries*. https://www.revolutionaries.com.au/calls-for-submissions/love-yourself.

5   Hazarika, N., & Archana, M. (2016, September/October). *The psychosocial impact of acne vulgaris*. https://www.ncbi.nlm.nih.gov/pmc/articles/PMC5029236/

6   Kendrick, K., & Isaac, M. (2020). *Mental health impact of COVID-19: Australian perspective*. https://search.bvsalud.org/global-literature-on-novel-coronavirus-2019-ncov/resource/en/covidwho-881427.

7   Cross, D. (2020). *Anxiety*. Harper Collins Publishers.

8   Davis, C. (2016). *Girls empowerment network*. https://www.girlsempowermentnetwork.org/blog/media-today-unattainable-beauty-standards.

9   Mahoney, B. (2019). *The obsession with beauty and how it is linked to depression in teens - Center for discovery*. https://centerfordiscovery.com/blog/obsession-beauty-linked-depression-teens/.

10 Wickman, G. (2018). *Love yourself: The message behind BTS's record breaking album Series*. https://medium.com/bangtan-journal/love-yourself-the-message-behind-btss-record-breaking-album-series-229119e81902.

11 Chapman, G. (2015). *The 5 love languages*. Northfield Pub.

12 BTS. (2018). Euphoria [Song]. On *Love yourself: Answer*. Big Hit Entertainment.

13 Lamay, R. (2019). *Korea's impossible beauty obsession*. https://medium.com/@ruthielamay/koreas-impossible-beauty-obsession-c97d92c4147e.

14 Cruz, I. (2020). *Self love through your five love languages — DIG MAG*. http://digmagonline.com/blog/category/self-love-through-your-five-love-languages.

15 BTS. (2018). *"We have learned to love ourselves, so now I urge you to 'speak yourself'"*. https://www.unicef.org/press-releases/we-have-learned-love-ourselves-so-now-i-urge-you-speak-yourself.

THE EMPTY CANVAS

Raneem Iftekhar

The world events of 2020 turned my perception of identity and belonging on its head. In the midst of school closures, plans abruptly cancelled and the world in the grip of a virus that knew no boundaries, the constructed version of myself, all I believed I knew, crumbled and fell away.

As I retreated into isolation, the months stretched on in the confines of my bedroom and telecommunicated meetings, where a struggle to adapt to a new, solitary, and colourless version of myself began. I found myself with only my thoughts and the seemingly never ending time to analyse my anxieties and fears that had previously been buried in the hustle of everyday life. The me who I knew before quarantine was eroded into a shadow that didn't know my name.

I was a student at a small high school that, in early March of 2020, had been preparing for theatre productions, games, and countless events. The pandemic cut through all our plans with cancellation notices and the frequent use of the phrase "unprecedented times". Staring at screens for Zoom classes, I scrolled through endless videos and images to feel connected to the world when it seemed the cord had been torn and broken. I was in a reality that felt dreamlike and hard to truly fathom. In between the monotonous video classes and the nights spent adrift in anxiety and sadness that sometimes bled into the day, I stared at the mirror and wondered how I had come to a point where I no longer knew what I belonged to and how to love myself.

In the midst of those long weeks that blurred together, one day in my Zoom art class my teacher made an announcement. Addressing our all-girl class scattered throughout the city in their rooms, my teacher informed us that "ladies, your next project for the rest of March is a large scale self-portrait". The painting was to be done in oil paint, in a realistic style on a 16 x 20 canvas. She wanted to see our life through our eyes and created by our hands.

I wondered how I was to do that when I felt like I no longer knew myself and felt like a floating visitor within my body. My mirror reflection was foreign and colourless to me. To put pencil to canvas, brush to vibrant paint, and depict who I saw in the mirror seemed an insurmountable task. As my teacher laid out the steps and took us through examples, I glanced at my shelves with the supplies I would need. The easel stood empty and daunting. The box of oil paints sat lonely and unopened, whispering that I was unworthy of their vivid colours. The brushes wondered whether I'd even pick them up. The empty canvas stared at me as I sat on my bed in a room with the blinds drawn shut, blankets in disarray, and laptop screen in front of me glowing with the split screen video boxes of my class. *I dare you*, said the expanse of pristine canvas white.

To choose a reference

Look for a picture where your eyes are prominent — the advice of my art teacher as I began the first step of choosing a suitable reference photograph of myself. Self-portrait painting throughout history was often a task taken on by artists voluntarily and served three purposes: self-expression, documentation, and demonstration of skill.[1] I was to fulfil all three purposes.

The process for my own portrait started with picking a reference. My phone was the immediate destination for the hunt to find the perfect picture with paintable lighting, reasonable angles, and an expression with character. 24/7 access to a camera as well as a culture of image based communication contributes to a high volume of self photographs in mine and every smartphone user's camera roll.

Despite this, I found it an unexpectedly difficult task to select a picture of myself. Scrolling through my camera roll in search for the perfect one, I relived the past year. Friends, family, parties, moments of joy. Pictures that were mundane but with their date, reminded me of turmoil and loss. To choose a single, frozen moment from the movement and current of life is a unique, often difficult task for any artist. Traditional art compensates for the loss of the ability to express the dimension of time by attempting to distil all necessary information into one singular image.[2] Yet the events and changes that had occurred in the months before March were so overwhelming and complex, that documenting their effect on me with a single image was an impossible task.

In October of 2019, the permanent closure of my school was abruptly announced, due to financial struggles that were not able to be resolved. We were told we had until the following June of 2020. Even if only for a mere two years, my school had become my second home. I spent countless hours on its grounds and gardens, laughing at lunch tables and complaining during early mornings in the library scrambling to finish projects. Long evenings I spent at debate practice after tired afternoons on the shuttle back to campus from tennis practice.

My camera roll reminded me of that in painful, vivid detail. My identity was tied to that community, it was apparent in the pictures I took. Now, sitting alone in a bedroom with that cherished community reduced to just classes on a screen that would also disappear come June and growing self-doubt and anxiety, my sense of identity had slipped away and I didn't know what to love about my isolated, colourless self.

According to psychologists, in the midst of stressful events such the COVID-19 pandemic, self-love, and the esteem you have for yourself becomes extremely important and acts as a shield against the onset of emerging, detrimental mental health issues like anxiety and depression.[2] I knew my own self-esteem was plummeting and fading from the place I had built it to in the first years of high school through new friendships and the courage to try new experiences. Now in isolation as weeks bled into each other, on a late night I read, through tired eyes, the translated song lyrics of a video playing on my screen. "So far away, if I had a dream, a dream of flying away", a soft voice sings to me.[3] My vision of the screen turns blurry, the tears come and I cry for a long time, the painful catches of breath and ache in my head taking over every sense.

For my portrait, I eventually chose a picture that is generic, a smile, pretty pose, and good lighting. It lacked a story. Yet, like my teacher wanted, my eyes were visible.

The underpainting

The first task of a well-executed portrait painting is something called the underpainting. A wash of a single colour, commonly warm sienna, fills in the vague swatches of light and dark onto the initial sketch where the shadows of darker brown hair and pupils are. Further watered-down pigments suggest the lighter tones of skin and teeth. Throughout history, classic art masters often used several layers of an underpainting wash to create a realistic painting with depth. The watered-down paint creates an impression of the subject, and will aid me in accurately colour mixing and placing the next layers. A ghost made of values of light.

My canvas sits in my room for the next few days, a slowly forming monochrome version of myself coming to life as I went through the cycle of sleeping, eating, and school every day in my bedroom over and over and waited for the moment when the painting began to look like me. It is said that one of the first steps to self-love is developing mindfulness of who you are and where you stand at the moment. It's knowing that your thoughts, your feelings, and current mindset deeply affect your sense of self-esteem and that without growth and a change in perspective, self-love is not possible.[4]

In an extensive recent interview for Weverse Magazine, RM, the leader of BTS, comments on seeing his life as an allegory to making art and that he is "waiting for the day that it all comes to the surface, like when you paint the base on a canvas over and over so the colors pop".[5] As I created that underpainting base, I was waiting as well. I went to sleep and her barely-there eyes look at me. I wake up and her eyes are still watching me. The sun sets and casts my room in soft oranges and yellows, the underpainting takes on an eerie glow. At some times, I wished I could leave it that way. I wished it could stay a ghost, only vaguely suggestive, and take on both the colours of the sky outside my window and the grey of my room. I wished I could accept and embrace the isolated, colourless version of myself. I wished I could look through my camera roll and not feel like the person I used to be was quickly fading and might be soon gone. I wished that my room didn't have to hold my emotions, my fears, and insecurities 24/7. Despite the circumstances and the loss, I wished I could love myself. The underpainting whispered that I was just like it, a shadow of my former self.

The first layers

The main part of creating a self-portrait painting is the layers of the paint itself. Squeezing thick oil paints onto my palette, I mixed them with turpentine to thin them and make them easy to control with my brush. In the journey to self-acceptance and love, patience with yourself is equally as important. It is the journey to a state of appreciation for yourself that dynamically grows and matures from actions that "support our physical, psychological and spiritual growth".[4]

I didn't think myself capable of that daunting task, I didn't think myself worthy to meticulously spend hours mixing vivid colours to give myself a "healthy glow" in-portrait when in reality I felt I lacked that. Accepting and having patience with yourself in your highs and lows is no easy thing to do and requires a full acknowledgement of the colours that often take over your mind, be it warm, bright yellows in moments of joy or overbearing grey in long periods of numb sadness and lethargy.

In the song *Blue and Grey*, RM writes that "words like "color" make me feel cringey, I feel comfortable with the vast grey area".[6] Staring at the vivid, squeezed-out paints on my palette, I wondered how I am going to create the hues of life when all I felt and saw was grey. I started the task hesitantly, playing with the oil paints to create the hues I saw in the reference image and using the advantage of its slow drying time. I often messed up, adding too much of one colour and throwing the balance off far from the colour I was hoping to create. Trying to reverse the mistake could take many minutes and the small tubes oil paint comes in means scrapping a big amount of it can be a costly mistake. My palette grew messy, my brushes and hands streaked with paint as I reworked the same three primary colours, white and black, to attempt to create the shades of vitality in a face. Then tentatively placing colours, I tried my hand at laying down layers and blending with the eyes first. Slowly, a version of myself in colour began to emerge and her brown eyes asked me if I knew her name. I stared at her and wondered if I could answer that yet.

In Jungian psychology, the psyche of self is broken up into several elements; one being the persona. The persona reflects the role of the individual in the eyes of society and is made up of the colours of their appearance and contribution to the world.[7] The persona is carefully constructed, a superficial mask. The persona is the broad strokes of colour that create you, the mere suggestion of what belongs where.

In my room, stood a vague painting — a replication of the persona smiling in my reference photo. In RM's song *Intro: Persona* from the album *Map of The Soul: 7*, he raps while surrounded by mirrors that "someone like me isn't good enough to be a calling, someone like me isn't good enough to be a muse".[8] To be both the artist and the muse for my own self-portrait came with similar thoughts to the lyrics of RM's song, as I wondered whether I could be my own muse. RM continues to rap that he has "regrets that I don't even get sick of anymore".[8]

Regrets seemed like all I had during those first months in quarantine, they piled up on top of each other and kept me up at night. They were at the front of my mind when I spent hours holding a brush and painting the layers of my portrait. Yet patch of skin by more skin, the portrait agonisingly and slowly came to life over the next few weeks. The entire process morphed into a form of personal art therapy, a psychological practice that has proven to help people of all ages improve symptoms of anxiety, build self-esteem, and help cope with illnesses, trauma, or stressors in one's life.[9] Technical skill is not necessary for humans carry the innate ability for creativity and whatever interpretation of colour and composition one creates as art therapy is beneficial to the wellbeing of their mental health. The artwork created in such therapy sessions are used as a way to explore reawakened memories and messages and beliefs from the unconscious mind of the artist.

While I laid down colours and blended tones, time passed by spent in a period of much self-reflection and analysis. Why was I unhappy? Why was I disconnected not just from the world but myself? Why could I not embrace who I was in my own room's four walls and accept that who I was before and what I belonged to was gone. What is the correct way to move on? I found myself asking, how do I make my portrait reflect who I am in a world where the lights, people and roles we project onto ourselves fell away? Where the persona of who we are is reduced to a small box on a Zoom call but the reality is actually hidden trapped somewhere deep in our mirror reflections in our isolated rooms.

Shadows and highlights

As the first layers filled in the underpainting, the portrait was at first two-dimensional and flat appearing. The portrait could not take life without highlights and shadows. A concept and method in art known as 'chiaroscuro' is the practice of accentuating the areas of a piece where light is present and where it is absent. Lightened and darkened versions of each colour mixture are used in a region of the portrait where the light captures the subject and where it casts shadows. Contrast is effectively created in this way, and slowly the portrait comes to life. Small, but incredibly important highlights are often just small dots in the pupil or streaks of light-toned paint that are blended in to create vitality.

In life, highlights often mean big successes and accomplishments. To me in the pre-quarantine world, a highlight would have been a tennis game won, an academic award or a party with genuine friends. In quarantine, highlights became starkly different. Small things taken for granted before became the only light in a day. A sunset. A video call. A Zoom performance of *Somewhere Over the Rainbow* by a classmate in musical theatre. A beautifully decorated pen pal letter arriving from another country. Things that often kept me less lonely from spinning thoughts and fully giving myself over to long nights of anxiety. These highlights sustained my long weeks in quarantine and when fully looked at in appreciation, they began to help form a new perception of myself.

Yet there is no light without shadows and there is no realistic portrait without the shadows needed to create depth. Jungian psychology defines the "shadow" as the hidden, repressed side of one's psyche that often causes guilt and discomfort with their identity.[7] In early quarantine, the shadows were many. The fears never left me alone, the self-doubt was a persuasive mould that was hard to shake off. Yet, like the way shadows are incredibly essential to create a realistic and compelling portrait, I have realised that recognising and acknowledging these shadowy emotions are as important for the process of coming to love myself. With the assimilation of the shadow, Jung writes that true self-acceptance and identity is found.[7] In the song *Interlude: Shadow*, Suga writes that his shadow will both clash with him and complete him "we're you and we're me," he accepts about himself.[10]

I paint in the highlights and shadows on my painting, blend them in with a soft brush and watch as the portrait truly comes to life.

The final frame

The final step of the portrait that remains is a background. The background in my reference photo is a nondescript, blue wall, so I chose to come up with an alternative. My immediate thought is to do a background of overlapping plant leaves. I search for the appropriate references and get to work mixing vivid greens and yellows after cleaning my palette of the million variations of yellow and pink-tinged skin tones.

Painting plants is always a go-to for me, something I find comfort in and find interesting to add to any sketch or piece. Frida Kahlo, the renowned Mexican artist, was known to regularly incorporate botanical elements into her portrait art and often specifically chose lush plants and flowers in her portraits to reflect her heritage and symbolise the meaning behind her works.[11] I have always found plants to be very beautiful and complimentary to many art compositions. However as a previous horticulture intern at a local environmental centre, I also see them as the ultimate representation of perseverance, growth, and celebration. The plants require layers too, yet they are forgiving in their shape and direction. As the painting's white spaces vanished and the frame filled in, the self-portrait sat on my easel, and with the 'persona' and 'shadow', a third part of my psyche began to take shape on the canvas.

A crucial part of the psyche according to Jung's theory is the "ego", a junction between the inner and outer worlds and the most conscious element of our identity.[7] The ego is both the awareness of one's internal identity and the person you appear to the world as.[7] It plays an important role in the development of one's full identity and can both positively build one's sense of self-esteem and negatively hinder someone by blinding them to their faults.[7] On its own, the ego can seem like the only needed aspect of one's psyche, but without the acknowledgment of shadows and the persona, the picture is incomplete.[7] In his solo *Outro: Ego*, j-hope explores his thoughts and mental struggles with fame and identity that led him to realise he has "only one hope, only one soul, only one smile, only one you, the definite answer to the truth of the world".[12] As I finish my painting, I realise that the smile of the girl on the canvas has a different gravity than the smile of my reference photo. The portrait's smile knows the long nights I laid in my dishevelled bed wanting to put the empty canvas back in my closet. Her smile knows the hours of colour mixing, mistakes, and frustrations. She knows of the times a Zoom call ended and I silently cried at the blank screen of my glowing laptop. She knows the tears I wept when the email that school on my campus would not ever resume came through, and the four walls of my room held the many regrets and emotions of anxiety and demotivation.

In the grey, messy room I lived in and went to school in, one full month of quarantine passes. At the end of March 2020, I turned sixteen at home with my family, previous plans for a large, sweet sixteen party cancelled like most other things. After dreaming of turning sixteen for my entire childhood, the actual day came in the midst of a quarantined new life during a global pandemic that challenged the very identity of who I was. As time passed and summer came quickly, an outdoor, distanced showcase was arranged by my art teacher on campus. It occurred in the last weeks before the school was set to close its gates forever. I attended and displayed my portrait in the place where so much of my fond memories, love, and friends for the past years had belonged. Where I believed my identity was tied to and where I had once had ambitious dreams of leading teams and running for class president. Those things are no longer attainable, yet when I returned for that brief day I did not feel like I myself was also disappearing along with the school as I had back in March. Instead, the canvas I painted with the colours of my own thoughts and dreams of growing independent ambitions stood in the display easel and declared in vibrant colour to everyone who passed by: *She had chosen to accept and love herself.*

Now in March of 2021, I sit writing this one year later after the pandemic started and I was assigned to paint that portrait. I am sixteen for only a month longer and the thought of time passing through my fingers with no heed of my hesitation to leave childhood can be frightening. Images of our school being torn down to make way for housing developments circulate around old friends. I look at them briefly, the loss still a bit painful. Yet life goes on.

I've decided to leave the high school system behind me and take a few local community college classes instead in the hope I can get an early start at higher education. With the surplus of time I have to myself, I finally made a long time dream a reality and opened an online shopfront with my art. My ideas and plans for it are jotted down and sketched on sheets of paper and in sketchbooks spread out on my desk that sits beneath my hung self-portrait. As my 17th birthday approaches, the portrait will surely be surpassed by time and become outdated.

One day soon I may take it down to shelve away and save. For now though it stays on my walls, as I leave my room to take a bike ride before it gets fully dark. A surprise new full version of a favourite song of mine, *Blue Side* by j-hope was released today and I listen to its atmospheric melody and the tinkling wind chimes as the wind rushes past me on my bike. The smell of jasmine mingles with the spices of a dinner a neighbour is cooking as day turns to dusk. At that moment, I know where I am going and who I am. I breathe in as the song fades. I am content.

References

1   Encyclopedia Britannica. (2020). *Artemisia gentileschi*. https://www.britannica.com/biography/Artemisia-Gentileschi

2   Rossi, A., Panzeri, A., Pietrabissa, G., Manzoni, G. M., Castelnuovo, G., & Mannarini, S. (2020). The anxiety-buffer hypothesis in the time of COVID-19: When self esteem protects from the impact of loneliness and fear on anxiety and depression. *Frontiers in psychology*, 11, 2177.

3   Agust D. (2016). so far away (Feat. 수란 (Suran)) [Song]. On *Agust D*. Big Hit Entertainment; Doolset. (2018). *So far away (Ft. Suran)* [Translation]. https://doolsetbangtan.wordpress.com/2018/06/01/so-far-away-ft-suran/

4   Koshaba, D. (2012). *Seven step prescription for self love*. Psychology today.

5   Kang, M. (2020). *RM "I spend a lot of time thinking about where I am now"*. https://magazine.weverse.io/article/view?num=62&lang=en

6   BTS. (2020). Blue and grey [Song]. On *BE*. Big Hit Entertainment; Doolset. (2020). *Blue & Grey* [Translation]. https://doolsetbangtan.wordpress.com/2020/11/20/blue-and-grey/

7   Jung, C. (1971). *Psychological types collected works vol. 6*. Princeton University Press.

8   BTS. (2019). Intro: Persona [Song]. On *Map of the Soul: Persona*. Big Hit Entertainment; Doolset. (2020). *Intro: Persona* [Translation]. https://doolsetbangtan.wordpress.com/2019/03/31/persona/

9   Slayton, S., D'Archer, J., & Kaplan, F. (2010) Outcome studies on the efficacy of art therapy: A review of findings. *Art therapy:*

Journal of the American art therapy association. https://www. researchgate.net/publication/241720286_Outcome_Studies_ on_the_Efficacy_of_Art_Therapy_A_Review_of_Findings

[10] BTS. (2020). Interlude: Shadow [Song]. On *Map of the Soul: 7*. Big Hit Entertainment; Doolset. (2020). *Interlude: Shadow* [Translation]. https://doolsetbangtan.wordpress. com/2020/01/09/interlude-shadow/

[11] Hirsch, M. (2015). *Visit Frida Kahlo's garden to see the plants that influenced her art*. Smithsonian magazine.

[12] BTS. (2020). Outro: Ego [Song]. On *Map of the Soul: 7*. Big Hit Entertainment; Doolset. (2020). *Outro : Ego* [Translation]. https://doolsetbangtan.wordpress.com/2020/02/02/outro-ego/

WAVERING JOURNEY OF SELF-LOVE

Destiny Harding

"Though I'm not perfect, I'm so beautiful
I'm the one I should love in this world"[1]

Introducing my narrative

Broad bodies, round bodies, lean bodies, long bodies; these days, it feels as if diverse, body positive imagery is becoming more prominent thanks to social media. Cohen, Newton-John, and Slater note that posts featuring diverse bodies numbered over 11 million on Instagram in early 2020, with most images presented in conjunction with positive captions and hashtags.[2] Despite this growing influence, unrealistic standards of shape and weight are still far too common. When my friends express their insecurities around their own bodies and appearance it is easy to encourage them to change their perspective into something more positive — to try to accept themselves wholly, perceived flaws and all, ignoring perfectionist concerns over what may simply be distorted natural imperfections. Although this support is so easy to show to others, such understanding and acceptance is surprisingly difficult to extend to my own body, a form of hypocrisy I have been unable to escape.

In 2017 I was given BTS' *Love Yourself: Her* album, whose songs I fell in love with and repeatedly played throughout my weeks on constant repeat. The energy and feel of the music was extremely appealing, and I was content with knowing that album and refraining from delving into their discography.

In late 2019 I became a fledgling ARMY, having fallen down the rabbit hole in the wake of BTS' *Map of the Soul: Persona* promotions in time to fully appreciate their end-of-year content.

I consider these two points in time to mark important periods in my personal journey of self-love, where in hindsight I began to slip into — and eventually out of — a mire of self-critique and mental ill health. Outside of the typical assessment concerns of college I had a happy life, yet it was all too easy to see food restriction as the solution to my poor body image and self-esteem. The feeling of hunger began to act as atonement for not living up to my unrealistic body ideals, and my successes in restricting my food intake were the valuable boosts to my self-esteem balancing my growing self-hate. Although at first these tactics seemed harmless, they created countless unhealthy habits and eating patterns that still sneak up on me at my highest points, waiting for enough weakness to drag me back down into that mire. Choosing between recovery and these familiar patterns of disordered eating felt, and continues to feel like, a never-ending battle. I am still trying to block out the disordered voice within me — the inner part of me that advocates for the unhealthy tactics and mindset I am trying to escape.

Scrutinising myself

To examine the sources of the obstacles in my self-love journey it feels fitting to begin with my relationship with academic stress, something that I can first recall feeling in high school. Consistently good grades were a steady boost to my self-esteem, and the possibility of a low grade for a class would spark, often unwarranted, anxiety. I was and still can be anxious over what ifs, worrying about the possible outcomes of a certain action and over analysing the reactions of other parties in an interaction. Even now I can still recall old memories of verbal scoldings or criticisms on my assessment that had sparked unwanted tears — although I do not think any fell, each of the not-really confrontations had hit me personally. I hated feeling like I had failed to meet expectations. These were not experiences I wanted to repeat, and as I transitioned into college I began a habit of unnecessary procrastination laced with perfectionism. I was either setting myself up for failure with unreasonably high expectations and critiquing myself in advance, or reluctantly pre-empting a sub-par mark and secretly expecting to receive something higher. Noordenbos, et al. describe this kind of relationship between critical self-evaluation and perfectionism as a common fuel for disordered eating behaviour.[3]

Over this backgrounded relationship with perfectionism came the slowly growing struggle with my body image. I always preferred sedentary reading over the majority of sports, and although I believe I stayed within a healthy weight range my physique was a point of insecurity when compared with the ideals I had in my mind — which in hindsight were based on fully grown adults and not wholly reasonable for my age group. I hated the size of my thighs and stomach, and the way their appearance under my clothes made me feel self-conscious. I avoided tight-fitting clothing and short-length shorts, generally trying to hide my abdomen area as much as I could.

Despite my worries, diets were something I had never considered as a means of addressing my dissatisfaction with my body until I joined a short fitness program for the summer. One afternoon the program's coaches briefly introduced the concept of tracking daily calorie intakes and finding an appropriate deficit to slowly lose weight. After weighing myself and calculating my BMI, I was unpleasantly surprised by my place in the index — I was not overweight, but it was close enough to make me uncomfortable. I originally decided to adjust this with only a light deficit, but soon found the appeal in further restricting my intake to see the number on the scale go down faster. Coniglio et al. point out that food restriction is quick to turn into an ingrained habit fuelled by feelings of accomplishment and control, and the rewards of successful weight loss and praise.[4] In chasing these rewards, I was unconsciously rewiring my brain and turning food restriction into an unconscious decision. Hobbs reflects this in her own experiences with her eating disorder, where her restrictive meal choices became automatic after constant repetition.[5]

My own restriction tactics quickly led me towards the weight goal I had originally set, presenting me with a dilemma — what would I do next? Was I safe to stop there? Maybe I needed more of a safety gap before I ended the diet, to act as a buffer against the weight I would surely regain. The idea of getting further away from that original weight was what drove me — I was terrified of regressing to that number, my mind viewing it and my body at that time with disgust and no small amount of hatred. I am not confident about digging into how much of that was truly warranted, but the image my mind had formed was certainly warped in some way. Brown et al.'s study on body image disturbance reveals how individuals with anorexia overestimated their body size more than their healthier counterparts, a trend that was significantly correlated with body dissatisfaction and drive for thinness.[6] There was also evidence that some body parts were more likely to be overestimated, along with the size or volume of certain foods — both of which I was prone to doing for 'safety'. It was difficult to tell what was reality and what was distorted by my mind, and through this uncertainty my body image and self-esteem continued to spiral downwards.

The perfectionist habits I had established with my studies came into play as my weight and subsequent readjusted goals crept slowly, slowly downwards. Although my ideal day would have involved little to no eating, as close to fasting as I could get, I was rarely able to achieve it due to the virtue of living with family. Coming home in the afternoon would lead to a family meal which I ate as normally as I could, and the opportunity to break my self-control and snack as much as I wished. Whether or not I went through with the latter, I would feel no small amount of guilt and shame after trying (and failing) to vomit up my mistakes. These attempts and failures would be harshly critiqued by an inner voice, the conflicted part of me that wanted to keep achieving these goals as fast as possible. Critical and self-destructive thoughts are three times more common in people with eating disorders than without, making up an inner voice that tends to appear in correlation with lower self-esteem.[3] Following these thoughts led me to try to compensate for my perceived failures through self-criticism and continued food restriction.

It felt like I was slipping into a fugue state — my thoughts slipping in and out of focus, and my mind disassociating from my routine of disordered eating. I made a habit of withdrawing from social activities to avoid affecting my progress, and constantly comparing and criticising my appearance in comparison to others. The Butterfly Foundation describes these behaviours, along with obsessive thinking about your body and changes in your relationships with others, as some of the consequences of a poor body image.[7] I made a habit of body checking and identifying the few areas of my body that I could comfortably love — seeking out visual and physical proof of my progress in exchange for precious sparks of serotonin from my inner critic.

Although these rations of positivity are the most prominent in my memories, at the time they would have been outweighed by the anxiety and fear after simultaneously seeing everything I hated about my body. In an attempt to relieve these negative emotions, I would continue my disordered behaviours and inevitably feel the urge to body check once more, bringing back feelings of disgust and self-hate, and slowly falling into a small yet vicious cycle.[8] Interrogating these feelings was painful and something I avoided, which began to extend to staying complacent and perpetuating my destructive behaviour; the situation felt inescapable. In search of hope, I eventually turned towards the solace of online communities.

Cycle of sharing

I had tried to keep the truth of my disordered eating, body image, and self-esteem secret as long as possible. For a long time the only place I could open up about my feelings and bitter emotions was online in a small community that was dubiously healthy at best. Through social media I had tapped into a network for those with eating disorders or similar patterns of behaviour, which provided me with optimistic stories of recovery alongside motivation and fuel to continue restricting. The online community was an anonymous place to vent without fear of judgement and reduced my feelings of isolation; I had a safe space that would respond to my negative emotions with acceptance and comfort, even if they were locked around unhealthy actions[9]. It was the only place I could open up about my frustrations with hearing diet messaging in conversations around me and through social media; my envy and desire to achieve the physique of various models and anonymous figures in carefully posed photos, my feelings guaranteed to be validated; the sometimes visceral desire to self-harm and vent my self-hatred physically, although I rarely followed through.

My regular visits and contributions to the community gave me external validation that semi-balanced out the negative critique I would direct at myself, but relying too much on an external source can become a bad thing. Studies have shown there are costs to pursuing self-esteem and validation from others, with the accomplishment from earning their approval only a short-term feeling that can lead to a vicious cycle.[10] Depending on the sources in question, especially if online or social media based, it is clear how this could cause negative long-term effects and dependency. Although I would eventually drift away from visiting the community, at the time it provided ample motivation to continue my disordered behaviour, and as I began hitting my weight goals they — along with my final, ideal goal weight — would gradually be lowered.

I eventually grew close to a borderline healthy/unhealthy BMI, and as I started hitting demoralising plateaus I began saying I would start to recover after one last goal was met. Around this time I could see some of the people I followed most actively begin writing about their own recovery process, and the weight that was lifted from their shoulders when they had finally committed, and I dearly wished to experience that for myself. Yet I was terrified.

The thought of physically telling someone about what I was doing, what I truly felt — my chest would grow tight and tears would begin welling if I began contemplating such vulnerability. But beyond that was the fear of breaking the illusion of a mere diet and giving up control over my progress; I would have to explain what I was doing, how I was doing it, interrogate the tell-tale actions that would no longer seem innocuous. To vent over text was one thing, but I could not bear to talk about it physically.

The final straw came after an appointment with a gynaecologist. At that point it had been around a year or more since my last period and my mother was concerned about my health. I had simply been enjoying the freedom of my life without the monthly hassle, until I was hit with the reality of what it could mean for my health long term. Amenorrhoea creates a gradual decrease in bone mass and compromised bone mineral density, and eventually osteopenia, especially if one has anorexia.[11] I never reached the weight criteria to get such a diagnosis, but disordered eating creates similar enough patterns when experienced long term. My restriction had made hypothalamic amenorrhoea and osteopenia my most pressing concerns, and I knew the possibility of other chronic health conditions would slowly grow higher over time. Through the Butterfly Foundation I came across Ashleigh's story, wherein eight years with untreated anorexia left her with chronic bowel pains and polyps,[12] and later Sue's story, where decades of avoiding conventional treatment lead to relapses and several chronic health conditions.[13] These stories hinted at the possible negative consequences I might be faced with in the future.

This new knowledge created an agonising limbo of indecision. What was I to do? I did not want to stop my disordered eating, but I was even more reluctant to actively create long-term health issues — that had never been my intention. Sharing my concerns in the online community lead to a surprising number of people encouraging me to reach out to... somebody. Anybody who could help.

In the week following the health check my restriction fugue began to temporarily lift, and I took the chance to draft an email to an online, free counselling service. It was just to test the waters and vaguely describe my situation to see if I was actually deserving of professional validation and help. My fears were founded by the still prevalent perception that you have to be sick enough or thin enough to deserve treatment, to qualify for a diagnosis that would open up avenues of support;[14,15] these feelings of inauthenticity or not 'deserving' recovery are extremely common.[16] Eventually I sent that email, using an alias and a secondary anonymous account, and it did not take too long for a response to come back. It was relieving to read. The counsellor's words made me feel validated, and I cried as I read their encouragement to talk about it more with a professional.

Eventually I did. I was anxious about the what ifs, the possibility of being rejected and having my fragile hopes dashed, but I still went to see a psychologist. I had heard about others' difficulties in going through multiple practitioners to find the one that was best suited to their situation, but I was lucky; the psychologist I saw was lovely and such a comfort to talk to, giving me no reason to look for alternatives. Profuse crying in each session became a norm thanks to my tears' association with vulnerability, but it was so very worth it. She encouraged me to explore methods of self-care in the earlier sessions, and gave and continues to give the support I am unable to show to myself. Through talking to a professional I could trust, I was able to share the burden of my secrets in a safe space and unpack what I was feeling — both benefits of reaching out as described by Beyond Blue.[17] In this case, asking for support for my self-love issues in conjunction with my disordered eating was an intimidating prospect, but it gave me access to guidance and an understanding third-party. Her perspective is free of the influence of a disordered voice, and I can learn from it to slowly improve my capacity for self-love.

After I had gone through a few of these therapy sessions, I semi-impulsively signed up for a storytelling workshop run by a national mental health organisation. Its aim was to empower people to feel comfortable sharing their stories of mental ill health, focusing on guiding the narrative to be recovery focused and helpful for the listener. Being so fresh in recovery led me to obfuscate some details of my story, but otherwise the truth was bared to my peers. It was cathartic to describe and share the majority of my journey in front of a same-age audience rather than a professional, and to then be validated in turn by their responses.

After hearing and sharing experiences with the participants, the whole workshop gave me a critical — yet temporary — boost of confidence to continue with recovery and allow myself to indulge in self-love; taking advantage of this safe space allowed for some catharsis, but my awareness of the half-truths would lessen its strength until I found a different source of comfort.

In his 2018 speech at the UN General Assembly, RM said "We have learned to love ourselves, so now I urge you to 'speak yourself'", encouraging ARMY to share their stories and have their voices be heard by others.[18] When I participated in the workshop I was not truly able to say I had learnt to love myself, but at that time I had risen from the fugue state enough to be in a better place than before. Through speaking myself and allowing myself to be vulnerable, I could benefit from my peers' feedback to see myself through a non-disordered perspective, as was the case with the support I drew from seeing a psychologist.

Both of these experiences would improve my capacity for self-esteem and self-love a little, providing a temporary boost out of the twisted depths. The external validation felt necessary to balance out my constant self-criticism, as I would be able to see myself through their eyes, even briefly, and find the reasons to show myself a bit of self-love. Baker describes using a similar tactic to help with her own low self-esteem, using the encouragement, compliments, and support from her best friend to see herself from a different perspective.[19] At that point she was unable to independently find worth and value in herself, and the support of a third party provided the foundations to increase her own capacity for self-love. Through a similar process I was using the perspectives and validations of others to try to find the value in the parts of myself that I hated, a method that was not completely successful but nonetheless effective. If they said it was okay, or that there was nothing wrong with it, I could begin to allow myself to say it was okay as well.

Over a year had passed since the workshop and my self-love journey continued to fluctuate greatly, the memory of the participants' words providing valuable encouragement. I had been rewarded for my vulnerability back then, and I committed to writing this chapter bolstered by my previous positive reception. It strangely feels easier to open up in a personal text that may be read by complete strangers than to speak truthfully to an individual or small group of peers. Perhaps it is the detachment afforded by a digital medium that makes it seem less daunting. Naslund, et al. have shown how this anonymous process of self-expression contributes to feelings of personal empowerment, a sense of belonging, and protects against societal stigma.[20] But going into detail about my ongoing self-love journey is still not an easy task; I need to be as honest and vulnerable as I can bear, writing truths rather than the softened lies that come to mind.

Opening up about these personal topics brings anxiety and fear of negative judgement, but embracing this emotional vulnerability makes way for positive emotions.[21,22] Putting my thoughts and memories into words becomes a little easier each time I try, and through writing my story now I continue to follow in my idols' footsteps by speaking myself once more. RM describes speaking something as an important act of self-respect, a way of manifesting a concept into reality by capturing it with words.[23] By speaking myself I am performing a ritual of self-love through deliberate vulnerability, crafting my message with focus and intention, and becoming aware of the scope of my emotions. I have previously attempted similar rituals through my attempts at journal keeping, but due to a lack of motivation and focus they were never maintained long enough to become a habit. In contrast, the prolonged time needed to write this chapter lets me see how sharing my story can be a soothing process, by softening the painful edges of my memories and making it easier to reflect on them truthfully.

Comfort from afar

Even before making the decision to reach out for help, I was finding comfort in reading the shared experiences and emotions expressed by other people. The online eating disorder community I had found acted as a place of catharsis, and the stories of recovery I had found provided comfort and motivation to strive for the same. Eventually, I recognised that the benefits of visiting the community were outweighed by its negative influences, and in late 2019 I finally found a new source of catharsis that would offer emotional comfort without the downsides — the diverse discography of BTS.

Music can be very powerful. Studies have shown that music can influence what the listener feels, eliciting a wide range of both positive and negative emotions and thus acting as a medium of achieving emotional catharsis.[24, 25] In particular, listening to mood congruent music can allow the listener to project their state of mind onto the song and relieve some emotional tension.[25] This is an effect I began to experience as I repeatedly dove through the variety of albums, mixtapes, and singles BTS had released up to that point, learning the lyrics and eventually developing a powerful emotional response to a few particular songs. With most of their music I am able to choose between vibing to the sound or being moved by the sentiment of their lyrics, but sometimes an emotional response is unavoidable.

The energy of the rap line's music has always been a guaranteed source of catharsis, and my initial encounter with this trait was through Suga's mixtape, *Agust D*, in particular the song 마지막 (The Last). I was extremely unprepared for the raw and personal nature of the lyrics and how it brought out a painful empathy on my first few listens.

"Sometimes I'm afraid of myself
Thanks to self-hatred and depression that came to play again...
On my first visit to a psychiatrist, my parents came to Seoul and had a consultation with me
My parents said they didn't know me well
I don't know myself well either. Then who would know? (Who knows?)
Friend? If not, you? Nobody knows me well
The doctor asked me (Have you ever -beep-)

Without hesitation, I answered that I have"[26]

Self-hatred and depression? Yes and possibly. Have you ever — self-harmed? Yes. Finding a reflection of my experiences so early in the song had me hooked. Listening to the entirety of it took me through emotional waves that almost mimicked my own self-love journey thus far — it begins low but ends high, creating a beacon of hope that I could aspire to replicate for myself.

"I only live once, so I live harder than anyone

Living half-heartedly can be done by anyone

My fan, my hommie, my fam, don't worry I'm really okay now damn"[26]

The Last was a raw comfort I turned to when I felt low, soothing the bitterness and allowing for a cathartic release of my emotions. Now when I listen, the emotions have lessened in intensity, but in the right mindset it still retains all of its power; with a playlist on shuffle the opening beats fill me with anticipation, and it is exhilarating to shout along with the chorus to try to manifest that brighter perspective for myself. It has been extremely gratifying to see these positive feelings shared by other ARMY in relation to Suga's open lyrics; in *I Am ARMY* both Lily Low and Sharon Chen share an appreciation for how the lyrics serve to empower the listener.[27,28] These shared sentiments help solidify my relationship with the fandom. Whereas previously I had used an online community to fuel my self-harming behaviour, in this new community my experiences were acknowledged and validated without being further encouraged.

Whilst I continued to form emotional connections to BTS' music, I was also trying to reduce my reliance on outside opinions for showing myself self-love. I avoided my abdomen and thighs but slowly started viewing my extremities through a positive light. My hands, arms, lower legs, sometimes my face — they were *not* ugly? Maybe nice? To bolster my courage and encourage higher levels of self-love, I latched onto the comfort I could derive from a lot of BTS' music. Rather than as a means to vent with, Trivia 承: Love in particular provided catharsis through tears and stirring of emotion. Although it was still an outside perspective, it was non-specific and comforting enough to feel like encouragement rather than a crutch. RM's masterful lyrics and wordplay, in combination with the emotional attachment I had already formed to BTS' personas, guaranteed some amount of tears would appear whilst listening to the song.

"I'm just a human, human, human
You erode all my edges
and make me a love, love, love"[29]

In Korean human is 사람 and love is 사랑, so RM is describing the ㅁ of 사람 being turned into the ㅇ of 사랑. Fan translator Doolset also adds that a person with 'edge' describes someone who is difficult and unsociable, which adds another layer to this metaphor.[29]

"What would be it like if I leave
If I leave, would you feel sad?
If it isn't me, what would I be?
Would it be that you, too, will eventually leave me?"[29]

As an ARMY the messaging in Trivia 轉: Love felt much more meaningful, and this is heightened when examining my feelings around it through a limerent lens. As Eaglehawk describes in *Idol Limerence*, limerence is an intense, unreciprocated emotion that in many ways precedes actual romantic love.[30] With components including intrusive thoughts around the limerent focus, fear of rejection and shyness in the focus' presence, and the ability to emphasise admirable features of the focus, these feelings are woven into the parasocial nature of the relationship between fan and idol, ARMY and BTS. Although I was aware of this phenomenon prior to entering the fandom, I could not avoid growing intensively attached to what I see of BTS' personas as a fan — inevitably beginning to cultivate limerent feelings of my own to some extent. Despite knowing the one-sided nature of my feelings, listening to Trivia 承: Love never fails to swell my heart with love whilst simultaneously draining it through a soft catharsis. Eaglehawk writes that idol limerence can be a transformational, healing, and cathartic experience, and I was able to use my limerence in order to advance my self-love journey.[30] This further demonstrates the power of music and the idol/fan relationship, as originally I was using the eyes of others to love myself, then the idol, and now through the idol I was able to start finding new ways to love myself.

I find that *Answer: Love Myself* plays a similar helpful role to Trivia 承: Love, the impact magnified by hearing all the members singing its touching message.

"You've shown me I have reasons
I should love myself
I answer with all my breath and all the path I've walked along
Yesterday's me, today's me, tomorrow's me
(*I'm learning how to love myself*)
Without exception, all together, they are all me"[31]

On the one hand, the song underlines the relationship between BTS and the collective that is ARMY — the feeling of making up a fraction of that is enough to stir emotion. On the other, the lyrics themselves reflect my own limerent feelings towards BTS and represent another milestone of self-love to strive for. When listening on a low, fugue-heavy day *Answer: Love Myself* is almost guaranteed to release sad or semi-bitter tears, but around the peaks of guilt-free self-love they become more akin to tears of comfort.

The three aforementioned tracks were singled out for the high levels of catharsis they provide, but it would be easy to list out many other songs from BTS' discography that follow suit; many ARMY have shared similar experiences of using BTS' songs as a conduit for self-love. For example, in *I Am ARMY*, Low notes RM's *mono.* album and the song *Zero O'Clock* as two sources of comfort during her struggles with her postgraduate studies.[27] Dissanayake describes how these rituals of musical behaviour create experiences that reduce an individual's stress and anxiety as well as promoting mental healing.[32] Tarr, et al. further confirm that listening to music triggers the release of endorphins and can activate other hormones as well.[33] By taking advantage of these processes, the process of listening to these songs has been one of my more helpful tools and plays a key role in guiding the slow gradient of my journey of self-love.

Coda

Vacillating between self-love and self-hate, reaching a satisfactory equilibrium is still a distant goal of this journey. Like a sine wave, my capacity for self-love can peak and dip throughout the day in response to the interaction of numerous factors in my life. There are high periods and low periods that can stretch for days or weeks, but with an optimistic perspective I would tentatively say I have been improving on a sluggish, gradual gradient. Yet I am still locked in a constant struggle with food, body image, and restraining my inner critic. On the low, fugue-heavy days, I regret ever turning to recovery and ruining what I had achieved — unable to love how my body has changed. The memories of what I had been able to do are bittersweet, and it is tempting to try in vain to regain those twisted feelings of self-love. On the higher days, it is easier to recognise what I have achieved myself, for is it not a strength to resist the easy complacency of old, bad habits? In doing so I experienced painful vulnerability yet also the benefits of venting and achieving catharsis in a healthier way. Sharing my story and tapping into healing music — I find that these two tactics truly help me feel more comfortable with showing myself love. I continue to work towards reaching balanced levels of health and self-love, and the comfort I derive from BTS plays no small role in that journey. From my extremities inwards it feels like I am slowly becoming more comfortable with myself — when in the right mindset and not scrutinising my reflection in the mirror. I have found a new source of numerical satisfaction after attempting to start weightlifting, with the little improvements providing the encouragement I need to maintain the habit. Through sharing my story here, I hope I have been able to provide a shade of comfort through describing shared experiences or at least illustrate some familiar and helpful situations. If just one person felt some amount of catharsis, inspiration, or simply a hint of empathy after reading this, that would be enough. It would make this wavering journey of self-love feel worthwhile, for then I can continue to walk down this path with others.

References

1   BTS. (2018). Epiphany [Song]. On *Love Yourself: Answer*.
    Big Hit Entertainment.; Doolset. (2018, August 9).
    Epiphany [Translation]. https://doolsetbangtan.wordpress.
    com/2018/08/09/epiphany/

2   Cohen, R., Newton-John, T., & Slater, A. (2020). The case
    for body positivity on social media: Perspectives on current
    advances and future directions. *Journal of health psychology*,
    135910532091245. https://doi.org/10.1177/1359105320912450

3   Noordenbos, G., Aliakbari, N., & Campbell, R. (2014). The
    relationship among critical inner voices, low self-esteem,
    and self-criticism in eating disorders. *Eating disorders*, 22(4),
    337–351. https://doi.org/10.1080/10640266.2014.898983

4   Coniglio, K. A., Becker, K. R., Franko, D. L., Zayas, L. V.,
    Plessow, F., Eddy, K. T., & Thomas, J. J. (2017). Won't stop or
    can't stop? Food restriction as a habitual behavior among
    individuals with anorexia nervosa or atypical anorexia nervosa.
    Eating behaviors, 26, 144–147. https://doi.org/10.1016/j.
    eatbeh.2017.03.005

5   Hobbs, N. J. (2018, January 9). *How my eating disorder became
    a habit.* http://www.fearfreefood.co.uk/fear-free-eating/
    how-my-eating-disorder-became-a-habit/

6   Brown, T. A., Shott, M. E., & Frank, G. K. W. (2021). Body
    size overestimation in anorexia nervosa: Contributions
    of cognitive, affective, tactile and visual information.
    Psychiatry research, 297, 113705. https://doi.org/10.1016/j.
    psychres.2021.113705

7   Butterfly Foundation. (n.d.). *Can body image issues be serious?*

https://butterfly.org.au/body-image/
can-body-image-issues-be-serious/

8   Side By Side Nutrition. (2020, April 7). *How body checking will keep you stuck in your eating disorder.* https://sidebysidenutrition.com/blog/body-checking-how-it-keeps-you-stuck-in-your-eating-disorder

9   Centre for Discovery. (n.d.) *How can creating a positive online community help those in eating disorder recovery?* https://centerfordiscovery.com/blog/can-creating-positive-online-community-help-eating-disorder-recovery/

10   Crocker, J. (2002). The costs of seeking self-esteem. *Journal of social issues, 58*(3), 597–615. https://doi.org/10.1111/1540-4560.00279

11   Warren, M. P. & Halpert, S. (2007). 14 - Bone disorders associated with primary or secondary amenorrhea. In M. Kleerekoper, E. S. Siris & M. McClung (Eds), *The bone and mineral manual* (2nd ed., pp. 63-65). Academic Press. https://doi.org/10.1016/B978-012088569-5/50015-2

12   Ashleigh. (n.d). *A decade undiagnosed.* https://butterfly.org.au/story/a-decade-undiagnosed/

13   Sue. (n.d.). *Never too late.* https://butterfly.org.au/story/never-too-late/

14   Lorna. (2019, August 29). *Confession: I feel like a fraud.* https://livingbeyondtheborderline.home.blog/2019/08/29/confession-i-feel-like-a-fraud/

15   Becca. (2019, September 20). *I feel like a fraud to my eating disorder.* http://beccasloveforlife.blogspot.com/2019/09/i-feel-like-fraud-to-my-eating-disorder.html

16   Jess. (n.d.). *"But I can't have an eating disorder BECAUSE...".* https://beatingeatingdisorders.com/2016/02/11/ but-i-cant-have-an-eating-disorder-because/

17   Beyond Blue. (n.d.). *I know I need support, but how do I ask for it?* https://www.beyondblue.org.au/personal-best/pillar/ supporting-yourself/i-know-i-need-support-but-how-do-i-ask-for-it

18   BTS. (2018, September 24). *"We have learned to love ourselves, so now I urge you to 'speak yourself'".* https://www.unicef.org/ press-releases/we-have-learned-love-ourselves-so-now-i-urge-you-speak-yourself

19   Baker, S. (n.d.). *My victory over low self esteem.* http:// clubfashionista.blogspot.com/2013/12/my-victory-over-low-self-esteem.html

20   Naslund, J. A., Aschbrenner, K. A., Marsch, L. A., & Bartels, S. J. (2016). The future of mental health care: Peer-to-peer support and social media. *Epidemiology and psychiatric sciences, 25*(2), 113–122. https://doi.org/10.1017/S2045796015001067

21   Grande, D. (2019, February 24). *Emotional vulnerability as the path to connection.* https://www. psychologytoday.com/au/blog/in-it-together/201902/ emotional-vulnerability-the-path-connection

22   Sutton, J. (2021, January 6). *How to be vulnerable in life and therapy.* https://positivepsychology.com/how-to-be-vulnerable/

23   Stokes & Friends [@stokesnfriends]. (2019, May 11). *thank u #RM #SUGA #JIN #JUNGKOOK #JHOPE #V #JIMIN from @bts_twt @bts_bighit -we include each in my finale #THEWORLDBLINKS . #BTSARMY* [Video attached]. [Tweet]. https://twitter.com/stokesnfriends/ status/1126962367835836416

24 Swaminathan, S., & Schellenberg, E. G. (2015). Current emotion research in music psychology. *Emotion Review*, 7(2), 189–197. https://doi.org/10.1177/1754073914558282

25 TenBrook, S. (2018). *Music and its effects on emotion regulation, emotional catharsis and psychological well-being* (Order No. 10809008). Available from ProQuest one academic. (2057678797). https://www-proquest-com/dissertations-theses/music-effects-on-emotion-regulation-emotional/docview/2057678797/se-2?accountid=8330

26 Agust D (2016). 마지막 (The Last) [Song]. On *Agust D*. Big Hit Entertainment.; Doolset (2018). 마지막 (The Last) [Translation]. https://doolsetbangtan.wordpress.com/2018/06/01/the-last/

27 Low, L. (2020). How BTS contributes to an awareness of myself. In W. Eaglehawk & C. Lazore (Eds.), *I Am ARMY: It's Time to Begin* (pp. 91–112). Bulletproof.

28 Chen, S. (2020). Speaking myself. In W. Eaglehawk & C. Lazore (Eds.), *I Am ARMY: It's Time to Begin* (pp. 157–173). Bulletproof.

29 BTS. (2018). Trivia 承: Love [Song]. On *Love yourself: Answer*. Big Hit Entertainment.; Doolset. (2018). Trivia 承: Love [Translation]. https://doolsetbangtan.wordpress.com/2018/08/24/trivia-love/

30 Eaglehawk, W. (2020). *Idol limerence: The art of loving BTS as phenomena*. Revolutionaries.

31 BTS. (2018). Answer: Love myself [Song]. On *Love yourself: Answer*. Big Hit Entertainment.; Doolset. (2018). *Answer: Love myself* [Translation]. https://doolsetbangtan.wordpress.com/2018/08/24/answer-love-myself/

[32] Dissanayake, E. (2008). If music is the food of love, what about survival and reproductive success? *Musicae scientiae*, *12*(1_suppl), 169–195. https://doi.org/10.1177/1029864908012001081

[33] Tarr, B., Launay, J., & Dunbar, R. I. M. (2014). Music and social bonding: "Self-other" merging and neurohormonal mechanisms. *Frontiers in psychology*, *5*, 1096. https://doi.org/10.3389/fpsyg.2014.01096

FOLLOWING MY FOOTSTEPS HOME

Shelley Hoani

Hei mihi (By way of introduction)

Every story has its point of origin, the source from which all things emanate and to which all things return and as an Indigenous woman, storyteller, and researcher, my story begins with me. In fact, Indigenous scholars Sium and Ritskes celebrated this as a distinctive quality upon which all Indigenous storytelling is premised, highlighting that "disrupting dominant notions of intellectual rigour and legitimacy, while also redefining scholarship [i]s a process that begins with the self."[1]

Not surprisingly, this process of starting with the self also resonates strongly with BTS' timeless and revolutionary messaging of Love Yourself.[2] Members of the ARMY fandom may already know and appreciate the overarching theme of this era, that began in 2017. Two key messages permeated throughout. Firstly, that loving oneself is a prerequisite to loving others[3] and secondly, that self-love requires courage; to face our shadows and to embrace our light.[4]

The addendum "Speak Yourself" emerged in May 2018 with the launch of BTS' Love Yourself: Speak Yourself international stadium tour. However, it became even more meaningful for me at the 73rd session of the UN General Assembly, held in New York City, USA. At this forum RM, the leader of BTS, delivered what I consider to be one of the most inspiring speeches of this decade. This excerpt from his speech is a testament to the type of person he is — caring, inspirational and sincere:

"So, let's all take one more step. We have learned to love ourselves, so now I urge you to speak yourself. I would like to ask all of you. What is your name? What excites you and makes your heart beat? Tell me your story. I want to hear your voice, and I want to hear your conviction. No matter who you are, where you're from, your skin colour, your gender identity, just speak yourself. Find your name and find your voice by speaking yourself."[5]

Thus, *Following my footsteps home* is an acknowledgement of my personal journey of healing and this excerpt above from RM's speech is the inspiration behind it. As you continue to read, you may notice that key elements from the speech signpost the pathway that this documented journey takes, guiding its flow and purpose with meaningful intent. You may also notice that at times I speak in the language of my ancestors, for I am them and they are me. This is not to disparage anyone from following along with me. As an Indigenous woman of Māori descent, from a small country in the South Pacific called New Zealand, I speak with the voice my ancestors gave me as well as the voice that I have nurtured over time. It is a wise voice, but also a shy voice. Once repressed and suppressed, it is now free to roam and explore like the curious child of my yesteryears.

Past: I ahu mai i whea? (Where did I come from?)
What do you mean I'm Māori?

As a child growing up, I lived with my parents, three younger siblings, and our nanny who cared for us while our parents worked. At the age of eight, my family moved from our beautiful, four-bedroom, seaside, suburban home to a small hydro town surrounded by pine trees, with a hard to pronounce name, almost 900 kilometres away. The new house seemed small and shabby in comparison. When the door opened, children of all ages tumbled out from its seams. Miserably, I told my mother I missed our nanny, to which she replied, "Your nanny is here."

At that moment a frail-looking, old lady came out, all bent over, her skin worn and wrinkled, speaking a language I did not understand. Supported by a walking stick that seemed to be an extension of her arm, she quickly herded the children into some semblance of order, and although still smiling, no one said a word. This was the 'nanny' that my mother referred to and with that realisation I cried again telling my mother that she had lied — this was not 'my' nanny.

This memory was my first formal experience of meeting people of my own ethnicity, Māori people. Fair to say, it was a huge culture shock. For the first time in the eight years of my limited lifetime I began to hear this word 'Māori' and it was being applied to me. Growing up, I did not know that ethnicity, race, or culture were a 'thing'. Even more shocking — the 'nanny' who lived with us and helped to raise us for as long as I could remember was paid to do that work, whereas this new nanny was my mother's biological mother, and as such, my grandmother by blood — Māori blood.

To provide context, Māori are the 'tangata whenua' of New Zealand, the 'people of the land'. As such, my ancestors were here long before our country was "discovered" by explorers, such as Abel Tasman and Captain Cook in the 17th-18th centuries. Rich with natural resources, many foreigners soon settled on our lands, including the British. Under the guise of maintaining civility, peace, and order the British Crown began a process of colonisation in the early 1800s; a process that would effectively alienate us as Māori from our traditional language, beliefs, and customary practices.

Growing up in this cultural and political environment, I quickly learnt that being Māori came with expectations of what is acceptable and what is not. Consequently, where school was once a place of enjoyment for me, it quickly became the bane of my existence, and remained so for the remaining nine years of my compulsory education lifespan. After learning of my Māori heritage, then being laughed at and teased by other children for not being able to speak this "foreign" language, I soon realised that it was better not to say anything at all. In fact, throughout the rest of my schooling years I worked diligently to separate myself from the culture that traumatised me as a child. In my mind, "that" culture and "those" people served no other purpose than to hurt and humiliate me. Unknowingly though, separating myself from my culture caused a big rift in my life and in the process of trying to protect myself — my name, my language, and my culture became lost to me.

No one called out my name[5]

For Indigenous peoples, names carry memories, serve as tributes to ancestral people, events, and landmarks or provide insights into the nature and character of the child. Likewise, in traditional Māori society "personal and place names were of functional significance . . . [t]hey were immutable, tangible markers of tradition."[6]

Who then am I and what significance, if any, does my name hold? My mother was always an avid reader, an attribute passed down to me. In my memory bank, there is a recollection of her telling me that during her pregnancy she stumbled across a book of poems; the poet's name, Percy Bysshe Shelley. That was how I received the name Shelley; with an 'ey' not a 'y'. My middle name was gifted by a female tribal elder acknowledged for her ability to heal by drawing on the natural properties of traditional plants. The name she gave me was *Waimaria* — 'Wai', as in waters and 'maria', a derivative of the word mārie, which means peaceable, harmonious, and calming. Essentially, Waimaria translates to 'calm waters'. Finally, as is the practice of a patriarchal society where the wife takes the family name of the husband, my family name became *Awheto*.

In hindsight, there is a distinct resonance to my name, Shelley Waimaria. In the darkest moments of my life, the life-giving energy of words, language, poetry, and the ocean waters would many times pull me back from the proverbial cliff's edge. Interestingly, English became the only school subject that I both enjoyed and excelled at. While I never bothered with the syntax of language, the semantics always intrigued me. As for my middle name, the fact that I was born under the Libra sun sign is as serendipitous, as it is destiny. Especially when one considers the healing and restorative nuances imbued within my traditional name, Waimaria, and the elder who bestowed it upon me. With regards to my family name — the number of times I was mocked and teased by people (not just children, but adults as well) who could not or would not pronounce it correctly, is testament to growing up in a society where cultural sensitivity and cultural responsiveness were not a priority.

No one called out my name, and if they did, very rarely was it out of care or concern, but more out of anger or indifference, jest or mockery. I often wondered how people could be so unkind in their words, mannerisms or actions; not just children, but adults as well. Yes, my name was Shelley, but as soon as someone found out I was born in Rotorua, a city known for its geothermal activity and sulphurous emissions, my name would quickly convert to "smelly".

Looking back, this memory seems trivial now, but I realise that this was only one childhood experience of many, each impacting my sense of self-worth, self-confidence, and self-love on a daily basis. Even more alarming, non-Māori people weren't the only ones doing this to me, out of ignorance or arrogance. My own people were guilty of this as well. I wasn't Māori enough to be Māori, but I was too Māori to be non-Māori. Over the years, this culminating belief of never being good enough, smart enough, pretty enough, and Māori enough continued, till eventually I believed with all my being that I was not (and never would be) enough for anyone!

Is this love that I'm feeling?[7]

Very early in life we learn valuable lessons that often stay with us throughout the remainder of our years. Some of those lessons become the basic building blocks of life; how to read and write, tell the time, tie our shoelaces, and dress ourselves. Culturally we may learn how to recite traditional prayers, take our shoes off before entering a home, and respect our elders. The commonality of those lessons is that they are preparing us to be part of a bigger community of people outside of our immediate spheres of influence. We are being prepared, if not groomed, to enter into society and as such we need to know what is acceptable and what is not.

There are other types of lessons though; the ones that come at a greater personal cost. These are often tainted with painful memories and emotions that motivate us to dig deep, find an inner strength, and rise above the painful experiences. At the same time, immobilising us to the extent that we become trapped, unable to move forward. As a result, we become lost to ourselves — unable to trust, to love, to speak, to hope.

By the time I reached my eighth birthday, I knew what it meant to be abused — physically, emotionally, and sexually. I also knew what it felt like to be betrayed — by my body, emotions, and those nearest to me. In order to survive the rest of my childhood and teenage years, I created an imaginary bubble, locked myself in, and tucked the key away safely where no one would ever find it. Feigning confidence, happiness, and innocence when in fact the opposite was true.

Growing up, no one spoke my truth and neither did I. Ironically though RM would, with these additional words from his 2018 UN speech — "I tried to jam myself into the moulds that other people made. Soon, I began to shut out my own voice and started to listen to the voices of others. No one called out my name, and neither did I. My heart stopped and my eyes closed shut."[5]

Present: E tū ana ahau ki whea? (Where am I standing now?)

Barefoot and pregnant

There was a time in my country's educational history where the "colonial state constructed Maori women as a group requiring domestication. Through education, Maori girls were trained to fit the state categories of 'wives' and 'domestic workers'"; a societal conditioning passed down through the generations like a treasured family heirloom from my grandmother, to my mother, to me.[8] Add to that a heavy dollop of religious conditioning which reinforced stereotypical beliefs of servitude to males, plus 15 years as a victim of abuse and it's not surprising that by the time I left high school at the age of 17, all I wanted to do was get married and have children. Mistakenly, I believed that marriage and motherhood (in that order) would bring me the love and happiness I so earnestly yearned for in my life.

Being barefoot and pregnant so to speak, became my way of life throughout my 20s and 30s. Although the term itself describes a form of oppression against women, I personally loved being pregnant with each of my children, bringing them into this world, and holding them close to my breast as I nursed each one. Those experiences and responsibilities gave me a sense of accomplishment, fulfilment, and happiness. Despite the ongoing violence in my relationships, with my babies in my arms I felt safe, I felt needed, and I finally, in someone's eyes, was enough. As a result, the voice that I had silenced and kept hidden within for so long, finally found a reason to be — in the cries and unspoken words of my babies.

Finding my name, finding my voice

To think that I spent my childhood and teenage years suppressing my own voice out of fear, then continued to do so in my adult years in order to survive may be difficult for some to comprehend. Yet, as I reflect on those years, not once did I deny the fact that I had a voice, I just 'spoke myself' in ways that kept me safe. My story, though, never faltered.

One weekend, after receiving yet another beating from my husband, I met with an aunty who lovingly told me I deserved more from life. A stark contrast from advice from my mother, who constantly reminded me that "I made my bed, I should lie in it." As a teacher herself, my aunty told me that if I chose this profession for myself I would always have a job, which meant that I would be able to take care of my children, by myself. It took five years of continually pleading my case before my husband agreed that I could go to university, and an additional five years to complete my qualification, secure full-time employment as an adult educator and finally, end my violent marriage. At the age of 41, I started my new life as a single mother and for the first time in 12 years our home became a safe haven free from anger, fear, and violence.

Tell me your story[5]

There have been many aha moments in my life; moments of inexplicable insight or realisation that led to life-changing opportunities. In my native language these are referred to as 'oho' moments (moments of awakening) or 'ako' moments (moments of learning). Even in my darkest moments when I questioned my right to exist, when I believed that the world would be a better place without me, there was always a tiny seed of something indescribable within me that refused to give in. While I may have given up on those around me and life in general, I realise now that I never gave up on the person who mattered most to me. Unfortunately, as revealed in this self-composed poem, I didn't know how to care for her and so she toiled through life, alone and lonely.

She$_{lley}$ existed,
but She$_{lley}$ lived silently, She$_{lley}$ lived in secret,
She$_{lley}$ lived in the hollows of untold stories, buried deep within

By 2006 I began to feel as if I had finally found a place of belonging, a place to stand as a Māori woman who also happened to be a single mother, an educator, leader, and Indigenous researcher. Personally, and professionally, I began to thrive. Gaining a degree qualification and ending a violent marriage were just the beginnings of my transformation. Within a year of gaining full-time employment, I had published my first piece of academic writing, commenced my Master's studies, and adopted a newborn grandson.

With the realisation that I had something important to say and a platform from which to share, my life took on renewed meaning. I began to share my story as an example of how education can transform the lives of an entire family and in the process, my healing journey began to take form. 'Mana Wahine' became the philosophical underpinning to everything I did, founded on the premise that all Māori women possess this innate quality. What then is Mana Wahine? While there are no exact words in the English language that can adequately convey the true essence of its meaning, there are many interpretations.

These are just two (of many) that resonate with my own knowledge and understanding. One of my mentors, Sarah-Jane Tiakiwai, interpreted Mana Wahine as "flickering flames of memories, scars, tears, thoughts, hopes, and dreams that you carry with you every day, constantly fanning them into your burning and passionate desire to leave this world a little bit better than when you entered it."[9] Indigenous singer/songwriter, musician, and documentary maker Moana Maniapoto described Mana Wahine as something that:

> exists in every woman, whether she is a flamethrower or stealth bomber, a plant or a placeholder.... both tangible and barely discernible, a particular mauri [life essence] unique to wāhine Māori that resonates with the mauri in all women. It is about connection – to generations past, to the land and to each other.[9]

When formulating my own understanding of this notion of Mana Wahine, I took my lead from Indigenous researcher and scholar Leonie Pihama. Over the years, her writings have informed my own growth and development in the domain of academia. In my eyes then, Mana Wahine exists because there are many who subscribe to the notion of 'meritocracy' — a western ideology that posits Māori as unworthy. In their benevolent voices they will tell me that in my natural state of being as a wahine Māori (Māori woman) — I am not enough.

That as a member of a line of wahine who descend down from Hina – [I am] not enough. That as a survivor of multiple generations of attempted genocide, as a survivor of this very specific battleground of settler colonial racism and patriarchy – [I am] not enough. That as a vessel for the continuation of our existence as Māori – [I am] not enough.[9]

Mana Wahine then, is my response. Mana Wahine reaffirms that in my natural state as a wahine Maori – I am limitless potentiality and I am enough!

Future: E ahu atu ana ki whea? (Where am I going?)
A seed born of greatness

> He kākano ahau
> (I am a seed)

> I ruia mai i Rangiātea
> (descended from the ancient homeland of the ancestors)

> And I can never be lost
> I am a seed born of greatness
> Descended from a line of chiefs
> He kākano ahau[10]

It took me fifty years to appreciate the wisdom that "I am a seed born of greatness", a realisation that came as I sat questioning the value of my existence, while looking out over the vastness of the Grand Canyon. Sadly, I accepted that I had been in a state of disquiet for a while, unhappy with my life, despite having everything that I needed. Subsequently, I also realised that if I didn't take steps to remedy this feeling, I would remain like this for another fifty years. Later that evening, while walking through the casino attached to my hotel I heard a song that immediately drew me in. I had no idea what it was or where it came from, yet somehow my friend was able to find out the song title and artist's name for me – *Boy in Luv* by BTS.

At 50 years of age, I fell in love with BTS: their music, their messages, their artistry, their flawless choreography, and their personalities. That 'remedy' that was sorely needed in my life at that time, had been found. I felt connected and inspired, but most of all, I felt like someone was finally speaking 'me' and my truth.

Loving myself: Speaking myself

To document my life as an ARMY within 200 words may seem like an impossible task, yet this next piece of writing is exactly that. These words were written for an ARMY project that never eventuated, however I am both guided and comforted by Suga's words that we shouldn't cast something aside simply because it didn't make the cut or we think it's not good enough. Sometimes an item's real value doesn't shine through immediately, because it's meant for another time and space. Grounded in my own sense of knowing, doing, and being this telling piece of writing, titled *My Many Tears*, is a conscious reminder of what transformation can look, feel, and sound like if we are courageous enough to take those small, but very necessary, first steps.

My many tears

I'm a survivor many times over; harassed, abused, and violated — all in the name of love. Victimised first by those who stripped me of my soulful innocence, then again by those who failed to protect me. To stay alive, I bury my pain, hope, and voice deep within; I'm only 16.

Within a heartbeat I'm 50. Painfully, I realise I'm still that young girl, shattered and forgotten, waiting to be saved. BTS enters my life, and the embers of hope that once lay dormant begin to reignite, but it will still take time to find my name and reclaim my voice.

It's 2018 and I'm 53, laying within the sacred embrace of an ancestral meeting house, receiving my 'moko kauae'. By birthright, this traditional female chin tattoo signifies my standing as an Indigenous woman. She carries the name 'tini roimata' representing my 'many tears'. As I take my first breath afterwards — the breath of my past, present, and future entwined — I finally hear my name being called.

Once I lived a life of shameful silence.

Now, BTS inspires me every day to speak my truth as an Indigenous woman, a wahine Māori — with gratitude, humility, and joy.

Te mutunga iho (At the end of the day)

Following my footsteps home is a journey filled with memories, lived experiences, and personal narratives. Home is where my journey was destined as this is the place that nourishes my heart the most; yet home is not a physical destination that can be programmed into a GPS tracker. It was, is, and forever will be, a space and place of belonging: 'ā-wairua nei' – spiritually and 'ā-ngākau nei' – emotionally.

Where words once hurt and imprisoned me, they now comfort and console me. They are unashamedly subjective, as am I, premised upon a lifetime of lived experiences. As a situated knower I speak with a conviction that comes from a deep sense of knowing. To be otherised and marginalised because of race, class, and gender is a reality for Indigenous women throughout the world, to the extent where we are "constantly having to 'try' and find ourselves within the texts of the dominant group."[11] This is why RM's words resonated so strongly with me when he humbly stood and delivered his UN speech. His last line, "find your name and find your voice by speaking yourself", will always be a bittersweet reminder that if we as Indigenous women do not tell our own stories, others will continue to tell them for us.[5]

On a more personal note though, those words are an acknowledgement that I am a valued being and as such, I should value myself. Just like fellow ARMY and author Lily Low, I now realise "that self-love is not blind acceptance. It is acknowledging that though we can improve, we still deserve to be treated kindly."[12]

My story is one of becoming – becoming the person that I was always meant to be. At the seasoned age of 50 years, BTS became the catalyst that helped me to reclaim this space – for myself first and foremost, but ultimately for my children and grandchildren. One day, long after I am gone, they too will want to follow their footsteps home. This is my road map for them.

References

1   Sium, A., & Ritskes, E. (2013). Speaking truth to power: Indigenous storytelling as an act of living resistance. *Decolonization: Indigeneity, education & society, 2*(1), i–x.

2   Eaglehawk, W. (2020). Exit the magic shop, enter the revolution. In W. Eaglehawk & C. Lazore (Eds.), *I am ARMY: It's Time to Begin* (pp.201-248). Bulletproof. Kindle Edition.

3   Wickman, G. (2018, October 18). *Love yourself: The message behind BTS's record breaking album series.* https://medium.com/bangtan-journal/love-yourself-the-message-behind-btss-record-breaking-album-series-229119e81902

4   Dyer, A. (2019, November 13). *Love yourself: BTS and the psychology of self-love.* https://medium.com/revolutionaries/love-yourself-bts-and-the-psychology-of-self-love-4afb9658f1f6

5   BTS. (2018, September 24). *"We have learned to love ourselves, so now I urge you to 'speak yourself.'".* https://www.unicef.org/press-releases/we-have-learned-love-ourselves-so-now-i-urge-you-speak-yourself

6   Walker, R. (1969). Proper names in Māori myth and tradition. *The Journal of the Polynesian Society, 78*(3), 405-416. http://www.jps.auckland.ac.nz/document//Volume_78_1969/Volume_78%2C_No._3/Proper_names_in_Maori_myth_and_tradition%2C_by_R._J._Walker%2C_p_405_-_416/p1

7   Bob Marley and the Wailers (1977). Is this love [Song]. On *Kaya.* Tuff Gong - Island.

8   Smith, L. T. (2019). Māori women: Discourses, projects and mana wahine. *Mana wahine reader. A collection of writings 1987-1998, Volume 1.* 39-52.

[9] Pihama, L. (2018, October 10). *"Mana wahine is…"* [Blog]. https://leoniepihama.wordpress.com/2018/10/10/mana-wahine-is/

[10] Tamehana, H. (2001). *He kakano ahau: Born of greatness* [Song]. http://folksong.org.nz/he_kakano_ahau/index.html

[11] Pihama, L. (2001). *Tihei mauri ora: Honouring our voices: Mana wahine as a kaupapa Māori theoretical framework* (Unpublished doctoral dissertation). University of Auckland.

[12] Low, L. (2020). How BTS contributes to an awareness of myself. In W. Eaglehawk & C. Lazore (Eds.), *I am ARMY: It's time to begin* (pp.91-112). Bulletproof. Kindle Edition.

ON RESILIENCE AND HOPE: LOVE YOURSELF

Keryn Ibrahim

This chapter was very different when I first drafted it. I had a complete outline and an upbeat ending, all nice and neat. It was about resilience and hope. It was about loving yourself, because that's what it says on the book cover. It was supposed to go something like this:

A student showed up at my office door one day, distraught and disheartened. She was a postgraduate and a former student of mine. *Over a year ago*, she reminded me, *you told us we can come to see you if we have a problem, and I have a problem.* Her problem was that she felt like she lost passion for her research, and she did not get along with her supervisor. This situation left her feeling disconnected and depressed. I invited her in, and slowly she began telling me the rest of her story.

In *Fly to My Room*, there is a line that reminds me of this event. "Let me fly to my (room)," croons V. "Get me outta my blues and now I'm feelin' brand new".[1] Somehow, that was actually what happened. It wasn't because I was a comforting presence, or that I had shared some wise advice that fixed her problem. It was, magically — and yet not surprisingly, because I have seen this happen many times — because of BTS.

In the midst of her tearful recollection, the student caught sight of a canvas poster of BTS on my bookshelf. Looking around, she saw plenty of evidence that a passionate ARMY occupies this workplace: the Season's Greetings desk calendar, a framed poster, more canvases. Photocards on a display block. Lyrics on my door, just under my computer monitor.

Encouraged by this, she tentatively shared: "Do you know, I think Jin's song *Epiphany* saved my life." Regular readers of Revolutionaries publications would know that in *I Am ARMY: It's Time to Begin*, *Epiphany* also came up several times as providing solace in difficult times.[2] I felt a sense of pride at this, at being a fan of a band that gave so much hope and kindness to so many who were lost.

When she left my room that day, I think she left feeling lighter. That is the magic of BTS, but really, that is the magic of their message: love yourself, so you can be your best self.

What eventually became this chapter, however, is something different. It is still about resilience and hope, and it still carries the 'love yourself' tag. Nothing has changed about the original story: the student did fly to my room one day and she left feeling, if not exactly brand new, then somewhat more hopeful. What has changed is me: I found myself in need of BTS' magic, and I was the one who needed to love myself.

I wrote this chapter as I was coming out of an anxiety episode. While I wouldn't wish this experience on my worst enemy, I am somewhat glad to have gone through it, to have survived the onslaught of toe-curling apprehension. The fortnight of crippling fear, dread, and exhaustion gave me clarity once I came on the other side: There is grace in sharing our innermost struggles, but especially in embracing and supporting the person who is going through such difficult times. It was a very humbling experience, and it gave me a greater appreciation for all the contributors to this book who wrote about and through their pain. As one of the co-editors, I had read every submission and marvelled at the strength and compassion of each author as they came to terms with the challenges they face — be it trauma, illness, erasure, racism, radicalism, and the loss of a sense of self and purpose. Reading them again post-anxiety made me empathise with them at a deeper level: healing and recovery are not easy or straightforward. It takes immense courage to be able to love yourself, despite it all.

I have always lived with anxiety. I have called it many things, regarding it as a persistent pest: monster, gremlin, Dementor. I was an anxious child who imagined nightmare scenarios whenever my father returned home late from work, the one who crept to my brother's bedside to check his breathing. Then I became an anxious adult, one who has somehow managed to function otherwise well. The severity of this condition ebbs and flows: I have gone many months with only tiny pinpricks of worry, but I also once lived through an episode that lasted almost two years.

This year has been an improvement over the last in many ways. We have settled into new routines imposed by the pandemic, and life has begun to assume the sheen of normality. When my family faced some health issues, which coincided with a few big deadlines at work, my downward spiral began.

Rationally, I can pinpoint the sources of my worry. For one, I have a wonderful son who is autistic. He is amazing in many ways, but his neurodiversity also means that many aspects of life are challenging for him and for us. I am constantly worried about whether he is healthy and happy, and nitpick at every perceived hurt or upset. Apparently, I am not alone; many studies have identified a greater tendency towards anxiety and stress among parents of autistic children.[3,4]

As if that is not enough, there is another axis on which I find myself vulnerable: graduate studies. I had begun my doctorate studies in 2013 in the United Kingdom. I took along my husband and new baby, and so we began our earliest years as a family in a foreign country, away from family and all that was familiar. I loved my university and my study experience there, but the combination of being a newly minted mother, moving halfway across the world, and an awkward start during the middle of the academic year, meant I began my academic journey on wobbly feet. That shaky start left a lingering lack of confidence, even as I gradually made progress in my degree.

When my three-year study leave ended, I moved back home with plans to finish my thesis in the next few months. Those lofty dreams were quickly dashed as we began rebuilding our lives, resuming work full-time, and getting our child a diagnosis for autism. All these time-consuming, important, and necessary events took a toll on my already fragile academic ego. In addition, being away from my university meant losing access to the resources I needed to do my research including regular physical meetings with my supervisors. I found myself in an isolated, confusing, and challenging time.

I am still currently working on my thesis. There is pressure from many sides for me to complete it: my employers, my university, but especially myself. My tendencies to be a perfectionist exacerbate an already fraught situation. Whenever I face a setback, which is often, or am uncertain about my progress, which is all the time, anxiety drapes itself over me. The structure of a postgraduate research programme, which emphasises independence in research and produces sometimes conflicting feedback from examiners and supervisors, provides a fertile playground for my anxiety to thrive. It is no wonder then that postgraduate students are six times more likely than others to suffer from anxiety and depression, according to a study that examined data from 26 countries.[5]

I am sharing these personal insights into my life not to elicit sympathy, or to offer any kind of excuse for the way that I have been feeling. Instead, I hope to contextualise how I find myself in a position where my life situation presents challenges to my mental well-being. At the same time, I acknowledge my privilege — I have a stable well-paying job, a loving and supportive spouse and patient and understanding families on both sides. Paradoxically this adds to my feelings of despondency: I have every right to be satisfied and happy with my life, and yet I am struggling when so many others are worse off. The guilt is the cherry on top of an unhealthy mental state.

At one point, sitting in my office and trying to breathe through the dread in my gut, I googled "anxiety + parenting autistic children". I read up on studies that linked this condition with the challenges that parents of autistic children faced in their daily lives, but it wasn't until I came across a paper by Neff and Faso that I realised what I was dealing with. One line stood out particularly vividly to me: "self-kindness entails being gentle, supportive, and caring toward the self in times of distress rather than attacking and berating oneself for personal shortcomings".[6] Other points also resonated, such as feeling like I am alone in my suffering, and endlessly ruminating on the negative aspects of myself and my life.

Reading that paper was like listening to *Epiphany* for others: a revelation. I have not been at all compassionate towards myself even as I tried my best to care and love for others. Mired in my anxiety, I transformed all my insecurities and setbacks into weapons of shame that I then directed towards myself. I have been viciously and relentlessly unkind to myself: believing myself an incompetent mother, an unfit wife, a failure of a graduate student.

When Wallea asked me to co-edit this collection a long time ago, I readily accepted because I wanted the experience and was eager to learn. We edited in tandem once a week in fun sessions where we geeked out about BTS while also reading through the contributions to make sure each could shine in their own unique way. I thought it was a privilege to read about the vulnerabilities of the writers, and the journey each undertook towards self-love and empowerment. I felt affirmed in my conviction that BTS is the best band in the world, and that the 'love yourself' message can help with the personal challenges that so many of us face. Yet there I also was, at the same time, wallowing in my anxiety and misery. Instead of beating myself up, I should treat myself with the same compassion that I would give others in my situation.

Breakthrough moments are also a turning point for the writers in this collection. For Jasmine, it was embracing both her fangirl identity and her revolutionary side; Gabrielle transformed her hatred of self into love; Rashifa finds healing through accepting that her chronic illness will always be there but cannot stop her from flourishing; Devin acknowledges that the racial discrimination and attacks he suffered are motivated by ignorance, and that he himself is loved and worthy of it, especially by himself; Brunna turns to BTS' music to heal from the trauma of a sexual assault, embracing herself and her body as beautiful; Cindy writes of rituals of self-care that help her weather any storm; Jacinta learns to embrace her inner and outer appearance and love herself fully; Raneem found redemption and resilience in filling in an empty canvas, both metaphorically and literally; Destiny finds a way to move towards self-love and heal her disordered eating with the help of story telling and BTS' music, and; for Shelley it is when she began to fully embrace her indigenous identity that she finally found herself, her home.

For me, as for the writers, realisation begets action. Action begins with the self. The ethics of care of the self often starts with an acknowledgement and acceptance of the pain and the struggle, and here once again, as ever, BTS provides some clarity: It is okay to feel despair. Their song *Blue and Grey* is a gentle refrain on a murky emotion and has resonated with many listeners because of its frank description of the loneliness and darkness of despair, of standing still and observing these feelings, and at the end, accepting them for what they are. It is okay to feel this way: this is a kindness and compassion that we all deserve.

The stories in this book testify to the importance of self-care, of self-compassion. But more than that, they have ultimately been about resilience, about holding on and moving forward even when life seems bleak and times are tough. BTS, who individually and as a group faced their own setbacks with the pandemic, understood the power of perseverance and expressed their hope that others would carry on too, as they sang so beautifully in *Life Goes On*.

Like an echo in the forest
The day will come back around
As if nothing happened
Yeah, life goes on (*Oh, woah*)
Like an arrow in the blue sky
Another day flies by (*Flies by*)
On my pillow, on my table
Yeah, life goes on
Like this again[7]

Finally, this book is about hope, about better times ahead. Sara Ahmed wrote: "Hope does not only or always point toward the future, but carries us through when the terrain is difficult, when the path we follow makes it harder to proceed. Hope is behind us when we have to work for something to be possible."[8] It is my wish that you too, will have hope and resilience in the good times and the tough times, and that you will Love Yourself through it all.

References

[1]   BTS. (2020). Fly to my room [Song]. On *BE*. Big Hit
      Entertainment.; Genius. (2020). BTS 내 방을 여행하는 법
      (Fly to my room) (English translation). [Translation]. https://
      genius.com/Genius-english-translations-bts-fly-to-my-room-
      english-translation-lyrics

[2]   Eaglehawk, W., & Lazore, C. (2020). *I am ARMY: It's time to
      begin*. Revolutionaries.

[3]   Falk, N. H., Norris, K., & Quinn, M. G. (2014). The factors
      predicting stress, anxiety and depression in the parents of
      children with autism. *Journal of autism and developmental
      disorders*, 44(12), 3185-3203.

[4]   Wang, J., Hu, Y., Wang, Y., Qin, X., Xia, W., Sun, C., ... & Wang,
      J. (2013). Parenting stress in Chinese mothers of children with
      autism spectrum disorders. *Social psychiatry and psychiatric
      epidemiology*, 48(4), 575-582.

[5]   Evans, T. M., Bira, L., Gastelum, J. B., Weiss, L. T., & Vanderford,
      N. L. (2018). Evidence for a mental health crisis in graduate
      education. *Nature biotechnology*, 36(3), 282-284.

[6]   Neff, K. D., & Faso, D. J. (2015). Self-compassion and
      well-being in parents of children with autism. *Mindfulness*,
      6(4), 938-947.

[7]   BTS. (2020). Life goes on [Song]. On *BE*. Big Hit
      Entertainment.; Genius (2020). *BTS - Life goes on (English
      translation)*. [Translation]. https://genius.com/Genius-english-
      translations-bts-life-goes-on-english-translation-lyrics

[8]   Ahmed, S. (2016). *Living a feminist life*. Duke University Press.

CREDITS

Bulletproof would like to thank everyone at Revolutionaries who worked on *Love Yourself*.

Editors
Wallea Eaglehawk
Dyann Ross

Copy editor
Mary Kinderman

Design
Paula Pomer

Production
Wallea Eaglehawk

Marketing
Federica Trogu
Wallea Eaglehawk
Catherine Truluck

Communications
Manilyn Gumapas
Wallea Eaglehawk
Yessenia Herrera

CPSIA information can be obtained
at www.ICGtesting.com
Printed in the USA
FSHW012334010921
84400FS